Electronics Repair Handbook: Troubleshooting, Fixing, and Extending Device Lifespans

Micah E. Zorn

Preface

Hey there! If you're holding this book, chances are you're either curious about electronics repair, frustrated with the throwaway culture that surrounds us, or maybe just plain tired of paying someone else to fix your stuff. Whatever your reason, I'm thrilled to welcome you to the fascinating world of electronics repair!

This book isn't just about fixing broken gadgets; it's about empowering you to take control of your technology, save money, reduce e-waste, and develop a valuable skillset. We live in an age where electronics are more prevalent than ever, but too often, when they break, they're simply tossed aside. This book is designed to change that.

More Than Just a Repair Manual: A Philosophy of Resourcefulness

Think of this book not just as a repair manual, but as a guide to a more resourceful and sustainable lifestyle. It's a practical handbook for anyone who wants to understand the devices they use every day, learn how to troubleshoot common problems, and confidently tackle repairs. This isn't about becoming a certified technician overnight; it's about developing a mindset of repair and problem-solving.

Why I Wrote This Book: A Personal Journey

My own journey into electronics repair started with a broken laptop and a tight budget. I couldn't afford to replace it, and the repair shop quoted a hefty price. Determined to find a solution, I started researching online, watching YouTube videos, and tinkering with the machine. It was intimidating at first, but I slowly began to understand how the different components worked.

After a lot of trial and error (and a few sparks!), I managed to fix the laptop. The feeling of accomplishment was incredible! I realized that electronics repair wasn't just about saving money; it was about learning new skills, challenging myself, and taking control of my technology.

Since then, I've repaired countless devices for myself, friends, and family. I've seen firsthand the economic, environmental, and personal benefits of repair, and I'm passionate about sharing this knowledge with others.

What You'll Learn in This Book: A Roadmap to Repair Success

This book is designed to guide you through the fundamentals of electronics repair, providing you with the knowledge and skills you need to diagnose and fix a wide range of problems.

- **Chapter 1: The Repair Revolution: Why Repair Matters** - We'll explore the economic, environmental, and social benefits of repair and discuss the challenges of planned obsolescence.
- **Chapter 2: Essential Tools and Equipment** - You'll learn about the essential tools you'll need for electronics repair, from basic screwdrivers to advanced diagnostic equipment.
- **Chapter 3: Understanding Electronic Components** - We'll demystify the building blocks of electronics, teaching you how to identify and test common components.
- **Chapter 4: Soldering and Desoldering Fundamentals** - You'll master the art of soldering and desoldering, essential skills for any electronics repair technician.
- **Chapter 5: Mastering Troubleshooting Techniques** - We'll provide a systematic approach to diagnosing electronic problems, along with the techniques and knowledge you need to become a confident troubleshooter.
- **Chapter 6: Smartphone & Tablet Repair** - We'll tackle common smartphone and tablet issues, such as screen replacements, battery replacements, and charging problems.
- **Chapter 7: Laptop & Computer Repair** - You'll learn how to diagnose and repair common laptop and computer problems, such as overheating, slow performance, and display issues.
- **Chapter 8: Home Appliance Repair Basics** - We'll explore the world of home appliance repair, focusing on safety and simple DIY fixes.
- **Chapter 9: Preventative Maintenance for Electronics** - You'll learn how to proactively care for your electronic devices, extending their lifespan and preventing future problems.
- **Chapter 10: Upgrading and Modifying Your Devices** - We'll explore the exciting world of upgrading and modifying your electronic devices, while also addressing the ethical implications and safety concerns.
- **Chapter 11: The Power of Reuse & Responsible Recycling** - You'll learn how to make responsible end-of-life decisions for your

electronic devices, emphasizing the benefits of reuse and the importance of responsible recycling.
- **Chapter 12: Embracing Sustainable Electronics Practices** - We'll take a broader look at how our choices impact the electronics industry and the planet, empowering you to make informed decisions that promote sustainability and responsibility.

Who This Book Is For : Anyone Who Wants to Learn

This book is for anyone who is curious about electronics repair and wants to learn how to fix their own devices. Whether you're a complete beginner with no prior experience or an experienced hobbyist looking to expand your skills, you'll find valuable information and practical guidance in these pages.

I've made every effort to present the information in this book in a clear, concise, and easy-to-understand manner. I've also tried to include as many practical examples and troubleshooting tips as possible.

Electronics technology is constantly evolving, so I've made every effort to keep the information in this book up-to-date. However, it's always important to consult additional resources and to stay informed about the latest developments in the field.

Let's Get Started!

Table of Contents

Part I: Foundations of Electronics Repair

Chapter 1: The Repair Revolution: Why Repair Matters

Hey there, future repair hero! Welcome to the first chapter of this handbook. If you're holding this book, chances are you're already curious about electronics repair. Maybe you're tired of throwing away perfectly good devices, or perhaps you're just looking for a new skill. Whatever your reason, you're in the right place. This chapter is all about understanding *why* repair is so important in today's world. It's not just about fixing broken gadgets; it's about joining a revolution – the Repair Revolution!

(1.1) Environmental Impact of Electronics: Our E-Waste Problem

We live in a world powered by electronics. From the smartphones in our pockets to the laptops we work on, these devices have become indispensable. But this technological dependence comes at a steep environmental cost. The lifecycle of electronics, from manufacturing to disposal, leaves a significant footprint on our planet, and understanding this impact is the first step toward finding sustainable solutions. The biggest challenge stemming from this is the problem of e-waste.

The Unsustainable Cycle of Creation and Disposal:

The production of electronic devices relies on a complex global supply chain that extracts raw materials from the Earth, processes them in energy-intensive factories, and ships components across vast distances. The mining of rare earth minerals, for example, often occurs in environmentally sensitive areas, leading to deforestation, soil erosion, and water contamination. Manufacturing processes use hazardous chemicals that can pollute air and water, posing risks to both workers and surrounding communities. The extraction of these materials has created a global imbalance.

Then comes the disposal phase. As consumers, we're constantly bombarded with advertisements for the newest gadgets. Rapid technological advancements and planned obsolescence contribute to a cycle of frequent upgrades, leading to a massive influx of discarded electronics – e-waste – into landfills and recycling centers.

The Toxic Brew of E-Waste:

E-waste is far from harmless. Unlike typical household waste, it contains a cocktail of toxic substances, including lead, mercury, cadmium, chromium, brominated flame retardants, and PVC plastics. When e-waste is improperly disposed of – which, unfortunately, is often the case – these toxins can leach into the soil and groundwater, contaminating our ecosystems.

Lead, for example, is a neurotoxin that can damage the brain and nervous system. Mercury can accumulate in the food chain, posing risks to wildlife and human health. Brominated flame retardants, used to prevent electronics from catching fire, can disrupt hormone function. These toxins don't just disappear; they persist in the environment, accumulating over time and causing long-term harm.

Where Does E-Waste End Up?

A significant portion of e-waste generated in developed countries is exported to developing nations, often under the guise of "recycling." While some of this e-waste is processed in safe and responsible facilities, much of it ends up in informal recycling operations with minimal environmental controls.

In these operations, workers – often including children – dismantle electronics by hand, exposing themselves to dangerous toxins. They may burn circuit boards to recover valuable metals, releasing harmful pollutants into the air. The environmental consequences of these practices are devastating.

Case Study: Agbogbloshie, Ghana:

Agbogbloshie, a suburb of Accra, Ghana, is often cited as one of the world's largest e-waste dumps. Here, mountains of discarded electronics from around the globe are processed by informal workers who lack proper protective equipment. The air is thick with smoke from burning electronics, and the soil is contaminated with heavy metals. Agbogbloshie serves as a stark reminder of the human and environmental cost of our e-waste problem. Studies have shown alarming levels of lead and other toxins in the blood of residents, particularly children.

Practical Implications and Solutions:

So, what can we do about the e-waste problem? The solutions are multifaceted and require action from individuals, manufacturers, and policymakers. Here are some practical steps we can take:

- **Reduce Consumption:** Be mindful of our purchasing habits. Do we really need the latest smartphone, or can we extend the life of our current device?
- **Extend Device Lifespans:** Repairing electronics is a crucial step in reducing e-waste. By fixing our broken devices, we can keep them out of landfills and reduce the demand for new electronics.
- **Support the Right to Repair:** Advocate for policies that require manufacturers to provide access to parts, tools, and information needed for repair.
- **Recycle Responsibly:** When electronics reach the end of their useful life, ensure they are recycled at certified facilities that adhere to strict environmental standards. Look for e-Stewards or R2 certifications.
- **Demand Sustainable Products:** Support manufacturers that design products for durability, repairability, and recyclability.

Moving Towards a Circular Economy:

Ultimately, addressing the e-waste problem requires a shift from a linear "take-make-dispose" model to a circular economy where resources are used more efficiently, products are designed for longevity, and materials are recovered and reused. This shift will require collaboration across the entire electronics value chain, from manufacturers to consumers.

(1.2) Economic Benefits of Repair: Saving Money and Building Value

Beyond the environmental imperative, repairing electronics offers significant economic advantages, both for individuals and the broader economy. While the allure of shiny new gadgets is strong, embracing repair as a viable alternative unlocks a world of financial savings and value creation that often goes unnoticed. It's about shifting our mindset from a culture of disposable consumption to a more mindful and resourceful approach.

The Direct Cost Savings of Repair:

The most obvious economic benefit of repair is the direct cost savings compared to replacement. Consider a cracked smartphone screen. A new flagship phone can easily cost hundreds or even over a thousand dollars. A screen repair, even at a professional repair shop, typically costs a fraction of that price. Doing it yourself can save you even more, once you acquire the necessary tools and skills. These tools and skills can be used over and over so the investment you make in buying the repair tools is a long term gain.

The same principle applies to other electronic devices. A malfunctioning laptop, a broken washing machine, or a faulty television – all these can be repaired at a fraction of the cost of buying a brand-new replacement. The key is to evaluate the cost of repair versus replacement, taking into account the age and condition of the device.

Beyond the Initial Savings:

The economic benefits extend beyond the immediate cost savings. Repairing extends the lifespan of your devices, delaying the need for replacement. This not only saves you money in the long run but also reduces the demand for new products, which, as we discussed in the previous section, have significant environmental costs associated with their manufacturing and disposal.

Furthermore, repairing your own electronics empowers you to become a more informed and discerning consumer. You'll gain a better understanding of how devices work, their common failure points, and the true cost of ownership. This knowledge can help you make smarter purchasing decisions in the future, choosing devices that are durable, repairable, and offer good value for money.

Case Study: The Rise of Refurbished Electronics:

The growing market for refurbished electronics is a testament to the economic value of repair and reuse. Refurbished devices are pre-owned electronics that have been inspected, repaired, and restored to good working condition. They are typically sold at a discount compared to new devices, offering consumers an affordable and environmentally friendly alternative. Companies like Apple, Samsung, and Amazon all offer certified refurbished devices, providing warranties and guarantees of quality. This increase in the refurbished market has created a demand for technicians and repair shops, thereby creating jobs and stimulating economic growth.

Building Value Through Skill Development:

Learning electronics repair is an investment in yourself. The skills you acquire can be applied to a wide range of devices and situations, both personal and professional. You can repair your own electronics, help friends and family fix their devices, or even start your own repair business.

The demand for skilled electronics repair technicians is growing, driven by the increasing complexity of electronic devices and the growing awareness of the economic and environmental benefits of repair. This presents a significant opportunity for individuals seeking a rewarding and well-compensated career.

Creating a Circular Economy for Electronics:

The economic benefits of repair are closely linked to the concept of a circular economy, where resources are used more efficiently, products are designed for longevity, and materials are recovered and reused. Repair plays a crucial role in this circular economy by extending the lifespan of devices and reducing the need for new manufacturing.

(1.3) Empowerment Through DIY: Taking Control of Your Technology

In an age where technology often feels like a mysterious, inaccessible force, the ability to repair your own electronics provides a powerful sense of empowerment. It's about moving beyond being a passive consumer and becoming an active participant in the technology that shapes our lives. It's about demystifying the devices we rely on every day and reclaiming control over how they function and for how long. It's also about challenging the notion that tech is some sort of uncrackable black box.

Breaking Free from the Black Box:

Modern electronics are often designed to be sleek and seamless, concealing the complex inner workings from the user. This design can create a sense of helplessness when something goes wrong. We are conditioned to believe that only specialized technicians with proprietary tools and knowledge can fix our broken devices.

However, by embracing DIY repair, we can break free from this "black box" mentality. Learning to disassemble, diagnose, and repair our own electronics demystifies the technology and reveals the intricate but understandable systems within. We begin to see our devices not as magical objects but as collections of components that can be understood, maintained, and even improved.

Building Confidence and Problem-Solving Skills:

The act of successfully repairing an electronic device can be incredibly rewarding. It's a tangible accomplishment that builds confidence and fosters a sense of self-reliance. You've taken a broken object, diagnosed the problem, and implemented a solution – all on your own. This feeling of accomplishment can extend beyond electronics repair, empowering you to tackle other challenges in your life with a newfound sense of resourcefulness.

Furthermore, electronics repair cultivates valuable problem-solving skills. Troubleshooting a malfunctioning device requires critical thinking, attention to detail, and the ability to systematically analyze complex systems. These skills are transferable to many other areas of life, from fixing a leaky faucet to troubleshooting a software bug. You begin to see patterns that would otherwise remain hidden.

Case Study: The Maker Movement and DIY Electronics:

The Maker Movement, a growing community of hobbyists, inventors, and DIY enthusiasts, exemplifies the empowering nature of hands-on technology. Makers embrace experimentation, collaboration, and the sharing of knowledge, often focusing on electronics projects.

From building custom 3D printers to creating interactive art installations, makers demonstrate that technology is not just for experts; it's for anyone who is curious, creative, and willing to learn. The Maker Movement fosters a culture of innovation and empowers individuals to create their own solutions to real-world problems. Makerspaces and online communities further facilitate this sharing of knowledge and support.

Challenging Consumer Culture and Planned Obsolescence:

By embracing DIY repair, we can also challenge the prevailing consumer culture that encourages frequent upgrades and planned obsolescence. When we are able to fix our own devices, we are less likely to be swayed by marketing hype or forced to replace perfectly functional electronics simply because they are "outdated."

Repair becomes an act of resistance against a system that profits from our constant consumption. It allows us to make more conscious and sustainable choices, extending the lifespan of our devices and reducing our environmental impact. We begin to question the "must have the newest" mindset.

Practical Ways to Embrace DIY Empowerment:

- **Start Small:** Begin with simple repairs, such as replacing a battery or a cracked screen. There are numerous online tutorials and guides available to help you.
- **Join a Repair Community:** Connect with other DIY enthusiasts through online forums or local repair cafes. Sharing knowledge and experiences can be incredibly helpful and motivating.
- **Attend Workshops and Classes:** Many community centers and vocational schools offer workshops and classes on electronics repair.
- **Experiment and Learn:** Don't be afraid to experiment and try new things. Even if you make mistakes, you'll learn valuable lessons along the way.
- **Document Your Progress:** Keep a record of your repairs, noting what worked and what didn't. This will help you improve your skills and build a valuable knowledge base.

The empowerment that comes from DIY electronics repair is about more than just fixing broken gadgets; it's about taking control of our technology, developing valuable skills, and challenging a system that often leaves us feeling powerless. It's about transforming from passive consumers into active creators and problem-solvers, contributing to a more sustainable and empowering future.

(1.4) Right to Repair Advocacy: Fighting for Our Right to Fix

The Right to Repair movement is gaining momentum globally, fueled by a growing frustration with manufacturers that restrict access to the parts, tools, and information needed to fix our own devices. This movement isn't just about individual convenience; it's about challenging corporate control, promoting sustainability, and fostering a more equitable and innovative technology landscape. It's about pushing back against the notion that consumers don't truly own the products they purchase.

What is the Right to Repair?

At its core, the Right to Repair is the principle that consumers should have the ability to repair the products they own, either themselves or through an independent repair shop of their choice. This means manufacturers should be required to provide access to:

- **Genuine Replacement Parts:** Available for purchase at a fair price.
- **Service Manuals and Schematics:** Detailed instructions on how to disassemble, diagnose, and repair the product.
- **Diagnostic Software:** Tools for identifying problems and calibrating components.
- **Unfettered Access:** No software locks or other barriers that prevent repair.

The Opposition: Why Manufacturers Resist Repair

Despite the clear benefits of Right to Repair, many manufacturers actively resist it. Their arguments often revolve around:

- **Intellectual Property:** Claiming that providing access to repair information would infringe on their patents and trade secrets.
- **Safety Concerns:** Arguing that untrained individuals might injure themselves or damage the product during repair.
- **Quality Control:** Asserting that only authorized repair technicians can ensure quality repairs.

- **Revenue Streams:** Protecting their lucrative repair services and replacement part sales.

However, critics argue that these concerns are often exaggerated and used as a pretext to maintain a monopoly over repair services. Independent repair shops often demonstrate high levels of expertise and professionalism, and consumers are capable of making informed decisions about who repairs their devices.

Case Study: John Deere and the Fight for Tractor Repair

One of the most prominent examples of the Right to Repair struggle involves agricultural equipment manufacturer John Deere. Farmers, who rely heavily on tractors and other farm machinery, have long complained about John Deere's restrictive repair policies.

Deere requires farmers to use authorized dealerships for repairs, even for simple issues, often charging exorbitant fees and causing significant delays during critical planting and harvesting seasons. Farmers have even resorted to hacking their own tractors to bypass Deere's software locks and perform necessary repairs. This case highlights the real-world consequences of restricted repair access and the importance of Right to Repair legislation for independent businesses.

The Benefits of Right to Repair: A Ripple Effect

The benefits of Right to Repair extend far beyond individual consumers:

- **Economic Growth:** Creates jobs for independent repair technicians and stimulates local economies.
- **Innovation:** Encourages innovation by allowing independent developers to create new repair tools and solutions.
- **Environmental Sustainability:** Reduces e-waste by extending the lifespan of electronic devices.
- **Consumer Choice:** Empowers consumers to choose who repairs their devices and to make informed decisions about their purchases.

How to Advocate for Right to Repair: Getting Involved

There are many ways to support the Right to Repair movement:

- **Stay Informed:** Follow organizations like iFixit, The Repair Association, and Public Knowledge to stay up-to-date on Right to Repair legislation and news.
- **Contact Your Legislators:** Write or call your elected officials to voice your support for Right to Repair laws.
- **Support Right to Repair Organizations:** Donate to or volunteer with organizations that are advocating for Right to Repair legislation.
- **Share Information:** Educate your friends, family, and colleagues about the importance of Right to Repair.
- **Vote with Your Wallet:** Support manufacturers that offer repairable products and fair repair policies.

The Future of Repair:

The Right to Repair movement is a crucial step towards creating a more sustainable, equitable, and innovative technology ecosystem. By fighting for our right to fix, we can challenge corporate control, promote environmental responsibility, and empower individuals to take control of their technology.

This is a fight worth fighting. By joining the movement, you're not just advocating for yourself; you're advocating for a future where technology is more accessible, affordable, and sustainable for everyone. Let's embrace our right to fix and build a better future, one repair at a time.

Chapter 2: Essential Tools and Equipment

Alright, repair enthusiasts, welcome to Chapter 2! Now that we've discussed *why* repair is important, it's time to talk about *how* to do it. And that starts with the right tools. Think of your tools as an extension of your hands – they're what allow you to precisely disassemble, diagnose, and repair electronic devices.

Don't worry, you don't need to spend a fortune to get started. We'll break down the essential tools you'll need for basic repairs, as well as some more advanced tools that you can add to your arsenal as your skills progress.

(2.1) Basic Toolkit: Screwdrivers, Pliers, Multimeter

Think of your basic toolkit as the foundation upon which all your electronics repair endeavors will be built. These three tools – screwdrivers, pliers, and a multimeter – are the essential instruments that will allow you to disassemble devices, manipulate components, and diagnose electrical problems. They are the bedrock of any aspiring repair technician's capabilities. Investing in quality versions of these tools will not only make your repairs easier but also safer and more efficient in the long run.

Screwdrivers: More Than Just Turning Screws

It might seem obvious, but a good set of screwdrivers is absolutely critical for electronics repair. However, it's not just about having any old screwdrivers; it's about having the right *types* and *sizes* for the job. Electronics use a variety of screw heads, and using the wrong screwdriver can easily strip the screw head, making it impossible to remove and potentially damaging the device.

The most common types you'll encounter are Phillips head (the cross-shaped ones), flat head (the straight ones), and Torx (star-shaped). Torx screws are particularly prevalent in smartphones, laptops, and other small electronic devices. For Torx, getting a set that includes T4, T5, T6, and T8 sizes is a smart start.

Beyond the head type, size is equally important. Precision screwdriver sets are essential for working on delicate electronics. These sets typically include a range of small sizes for each head type, allowing you to find the perfect fit for even the tiniest screws. Look for sets with swivel heads or rotating caps, as these make it much easier to apply consistent pressure and avoid stripping the screw.

A crucial feature to consider is *magnetic tips*. These are an absolute lifesaver when working with small screws, preventing them from falling into hard-to-reach places and saving you a lot of frustration. Some screwdriver sets come with interchangeable magnetic tips, allowing you to customize your screwdrivers for different tasks.

When choosing screwdrivers, look for comfortable handles that provide a good grip. Ergonomic handles can reduce hand fatigue, especially during long repair sessions. Also, consider the material of the screwdriver shaft. Chrome vanadium steel is a durable and rust-resistant option that will ensure your screwdrivers last for years to come.

Pliers: Gripping, Bending, and Cutting with Precision

Pliers are another essential tool for electronics repair, used for gripping, bending, and cutting wires and components. Like screwdrivers, there are different types of pliers designed for specific tasks.

Needle-nose pliers are invaluable for reaching into tight spaces and manipulating small components. Wire cutters are essential for cleanly cutting wires and component leads. Diagonal cutting pliers, also known as "dikes," are used for flush-cutting component leads close to a circuit board.

When choosing pliers, look for comfortable, insulated handles that provide a secure grip. Insulated handles are particularly important for safety, as they protect you from electrical shock. Also, consider the quality of the cutting edges. Sharp, precise cutting edges will make your work easier and prevent damage to wires and components.

The Multimeter: Your Electrical Detective

The multimeter is arguably the most important tool in your basic toolkit. It's your electrical detective, allowing you to measure voltage, current, and resistance – the fundamental properties of electricity. Understanding these properties is essential for diagnosing electronic problems and verifying the functionality of components.

Digital multimeters (DMMs) are the most common type, offering a digital display for easy reading. When choosing a DMM, look for the following features:

- **Voltage Measurement:** Capable of measuring both AC and DC voltage.
- **Current Measurement:** Capable of measuring both AC and DC current.
- **Resistance Measurement:** Measures the resistance of components and circuits.
- **Continuity Testing:** A must-have feature that allows you to check for broken wires or short circuits. The multimeter will beep when there is a complete circuit.
- **Diode Testing:** Used to check the functionality of diodes and other semiconductors.

Some multimeters also offer additional features, such as capacitance measurement, frequency measurement, and temperature measurement. While these features can be useful, they are not essential for basic electronics repair.

A crucial safety feature is overload protection. This protects the multimeter from damage if you accidentally measure a voltage or current that is too high. Also, make sure the multimeter is properly rated for the voltage and current levels you will be working with.

When using a multimeter, always follow safety precautions. Never measure voltage on a live circuit unless you are properly trained and understand the risks involved.

Investing in a quality multimeter is an investment in your repair skills. It will allow you to diagnose problems quickly and accurately, saving you time and frustration.

Choosing Quality Over Quantity

When it comes to your basic toolkit, it's better to invest in quality tools rather than buying a cheap set with a lot of pieces. Quality tools will last longer, perform better, and make your repairs easier and safer. Start with a few essential tools and gradually add more specialized tools as your skills and needs grow.

With a solid basic toolkit in hand, you'll be well-equipped to tackle a wide range of electronics repair projects. In the next section, we'll delve into the world of soldering and desoldering, adding another essential skill to your repertoire.

(2.2) Soldering Station Essentials: Iron, Solder, Flux

Soldering is a fundamental skill in electronics repair, allowing you to create durable and reliable electrical connections. To master this skill, you'll need the right tools, and at the heart of soldering lies the soldering station, comprising three essential elements: the soldering iron, the solder itself, and flux. Think of these three as a team, working together to ensure clean, strong, and effective connections.

The Soldering Iron: Your Heat Source, Your Precision Instrument

The soldering iron is the core of your soldering station. It's much more than just a heated stick; it's a precision instrument that allows you to apply heat precisely where you need it, melting solder and creating a permanent bond between components and circuit boards. Choosing the right soldering iron is crucial for both efficiency and safety.

One of the most important factors to consider is temperature control. A soldering iron with adjustable temperature control is highly recommended, as different components and solders require different temperatures. Too much heat can damage sensitive components, while too little heat can result in a poor solder joint. Look for soldering irons with a temperature range of at least 200°C to 450°C (392°F to 842°F).

Wattage is another key consideration. A wattage of 30-60 watts is generally sufficient for most electronics work. Higher wattage irons heat up faster and can maintain their temperature better, but they can also be more prone to overheating sensitive components if you're not careful.

The shape of the soldering iron tip also plays a crucial role. Different tip shapes are designed for different tasks. A conical tip is a good all-around choice for general soldering. Chisel tips are useful for soldering larger components or surface-mount devices. Fine-point tips are ideal for soldering very small components in tight spaces.

Soldering stations often come with additional features, such as a built-in stand, a cleaning sponge, and a digital display showing the current temperature. These features can enhance your soldering experience and make your work more efficient.

Investing in a quality soldering iron from a reputable brand is a worthwhile investment. A well-built soldering iron will last for years and provide consistent performance.

Solder: The Bonding Agent, the Bridge Between Components

Solder is the metallic alloy used to create the electrical and mechanical connection between components. It's the "glue" that holds everything together. While there are different types of solder available, rosin-core solder is the most common choice for electronics work.

Rosin-core solder contains flux in its core, which helps to clean the surfaces being soldered and promote a strong bond. The flux melts and flows onto the surfaces being joined, removing oxidation and contaminants.

The diameter of the solder wire is also important. A solder diameter of 0.8mm or 1mm is a good choice for most electronics applications. Smaller diameter solder is easier to control and allows for more precise soldering.

Lead-free solder is becoming increasingly popular due to environmental concerns. While lead-free solder is more environmentally friendly, it can be more difficult to work with than traditional lead-based solder. It requires higher temperatures and tends to form a less shiny joint. If you're just starting out, lead-based solder may be easier to learn with, but be sure to follow proper safety precautions (wash your hands thoroughly after handling solder).

Flux: The Cleaning Power, Ensuring a Strong Bond

Flux is a chemical cleaning agent that is essential for successful soldering. It removes oxidation and other contaminants from the surfaces being soldered, allowing the solder to flow smoothly and create a strong, reliable connection.

Without flux, solder will not adhere properly to the surfaces, resulting in a weak or unreliable joint. Flux comes in various forms, including liquid, paste, and pen. Rosin flux is a common choice for electronics work, as it is non-corrosive and easy to clean.

Flux pens are a convenient way to apply flux precisely to the area being soldered. They dispense a small amount of liquid flux, allowing for controlled application and minimizing mess.

When using flux, be sure to apply it sparingly. Too much flux can create a mess and leave a residue that can attract dirt and moisture. After soldering, clean the area with isopropyl alcohol to remove any remaining flux residue.

Creating the Perfect Solder Joint: A Symphony of Elements

The key to successful soldering is to use the right tools and techniques. Ensure your soldering iron is clean and properly tinned (coated with a thin layer of solder). Apply a small amount of flux to the surfaces being soldered. Heat the surfaces with the soldering iron, and then apply solder to the heated surfaces. Allow the solder to flow smoothly and form a shiny, concave joint.

Avoid overheating the solder joint, as this can damage components and weaken the connection. Also, avoid using too much solder, as this can create a messy and unreliable joint.

With practice and patience, you'll develop the skills to create perfect solder joints every time. Soldering becomes almost second nature with enough practice. The proper soldering station makes this easier and safer.

The soldering station, composed of the iron, solder, and flux, is a cornerstone of electronics repair. Investing in quality components and mastering the art of soldering will unlock a world of possibilities, allowing you to repair, modify, and create your own electronic devices.

(2.3) Advanced Tools: Heat Gun, Oscilloscope (Overview)

As your electronics repair skills evolve, you'll eventually encounter situations that require more specialized tools. While a basic toolkit will get you far, adding a heat gun and an oscilloscope (even with a basic understanding of its functionality) can significantly expand your capabilities and allow you to tackle more complex repairs and diagnostics. These are the tools that separate the enthusiastic hobbyist from the more advanced technician. This section serves as an introduction; entire books are dedicated to mastering these devices.

The Heat Gun: More Than Just Hot Air

A heat gun is a versatile tool that emits a stream of hot air, used for a variety of tasks in electronics repair. It's not a replacement for a soldering iron, but rather a complementary tool that can be used for tasks that a soldering iron can't handle.

One of the most common applications for a heat gun is desoldering surface-mount components (SMDs). SMDs are small components that are soldered directly onto the surface of a circuit board, without any leads extending through holes. Removing SMDs with a soldering iron can be difficult and time-consuming, but a heat gun can quickly and easily melt the solder on all the pins simultaneously, allowing you to lift the component off the board.

Heat guns are also useful for shrinking heat shrink tubing, which is used to insulate wires and connections. Simply slide the heat shrink tubing over the connection and apply heat with the heat gun until the tubing shrinks tightly around the wires.

Other applications for a heat gun include removing stickers and labels, softening adhesives, and even reflowing solder on entire circuit boards (in specialized situations).

When choosing a heat gun for electronics repair, look for one with adjustable temperature and airflow settings. This will allow you to control the amount of heat being applied and prevent damage to sensitive components. Also, consider the size and shape of the nozzle. A small, focused nozzle is ideal for working on delicate electronics.

Safety is paramount when using a heat gun. Always wear safety glasses to protect your eyes from hot air and debris. Work in a well-ventilated area to avoid inhaling fumes. Be careful not to overheat components, as this can cause them to fail.

The heat gun opens up a world of possibilities for electronics repair, allowing you to tackle tasks that would be impossible with a soldering iron alone. It expands your reach to include newer technologies.

The Oscilloscope: Visualizing the Invisible Signals

The oscilloscope is a powerful tool that allows you to visualize electrical signals. It displays a graph of voltage versus time, showing you the shape, frequency, and amplitude of the signal. Understanding these properties is essential for diagnosing complex circuit problems and troubleshooting digital circuits.

While oscilloscopes can be expensive and complex to use, even a basic understanding of their functionality can be invaluable for electronics repair.

Oscilloscopes are particularly useful for troubleshooting digital circuits. By examining the shape and timing of digital signals, you can identify timing problems, logic errors, and other issues that would be difficult to detect with a multimeter alone. For example, you can verify the clock signal frequency, check for signal integrity issues, and identify glitches or noise on the signal.

Oscilloscopes are also useful for analyzing analog signals. By examining the shape and amplitude of analog signals, you can identify distortion, noise, and other problems that can affect circuit performance.

When choosing an oscilloscope for electronics repair, consider the following factors:

- **Bandwidth:** The maximum frequency that the oscilloscope can accurately measure. A bandwidth of at least 100 MHz is recommended for general-purpose electronics repair.
- **Sample Rate:** The number of samples per second that the oscilloscope can acquire. A higher sample rate allows you to capture faster signals more accurately.
- **Number of Channels:** The number of signals that the oscilloscope can display simultaneously. Two or four channels are typically sufficient for most electronics repair applications.
- **Digital Storage Oscilloscope (DSO):** Most modern oscilloscopes are DSOs, which store the captured signal digitally and allow you to analyze it in detail.

- **Portability:** USB-based oscilloscopes are great for portability.

Learning to use an oscilloscope takes time and practice, but the rewards are well worth the effort. It's like learning to read another language, except instead of words, you're reading electrical signals.

These Aren't Entry Level Tools

While these tools are incredibly powerful, it's important to recognize that they are not essential for basic electronics repair. Start with the basic toolkit and gradually add these tools as your skills and needs grow. Learning to use a multimeter effectively is a crucial first step before venturing into the world of oscilloscopes. They can easily be used incorrectly if you don't have a firm grasp of electronics basics.

However, with a heat gun and an oscilloscope in your arsenal, you'll be well-equipped to tackle even the most challenging electronics repair projects. These tools expand your diagnostic capabilities and open up new possibilities for repairing and modifying electronic devices.

(2.4) Tool Selection Guide: Matching Tools to Tasks

Having a well-stocked toolkit is only half the battle. Knowing *which* tool to use for *which* task is just as important. Using the wrong tool can lead to frustration, wasted time, and even damage to the device you're trying to repair. This section is designed to be your guide in navigating your toolkit, ensuring you choose the right instrument for the job, every time. Think of it as learning the language of your tools and how they speak to the delicate components you're working with.

The Right Tool for the Right Screw: Preventing Stripped Heads

One of the most common mistakes in electronics repair is using the wrong screwdriver. As we discussed earlier, there are many different types of screw heads, and using the wrong screwdriver can easily strip the screw head, making it impossible to remove.

For example, using a Phillips head screwdriver on a Pozidriv screw (which looks similar to a Phillips head) can quickly damage the screw head. Likewise, using a screwdriver that is too large or too small for the screw head can also lead to stripping.

Before attempting to remove a screw, carefully examine the screw head to determine the type and size of screwdriver needed. Use a precision screwdriver set to find the perfect fit. Apply firm, consistent pressure while turning the screwdriver, and avoid using excessive force. If the screw is particularly tight, try using a penetrating oil to loosen it before attempting to remove it.

Gentle Disassembly: Avoiding Damage to Cases and Connectors

Disassembling electronic devices can be tricky, especially if you're not familiar with the device's construction. Applying too much force can easily damage plastic cases, break connectors, or even crack circuit boards.

Plastic opening tools, such as spudgers and picks, are essential for gently prying open cases and disconnecting connectors. These tools are made of soft plastic that won't scratch or damage the device.

When disassembling a device, take your time and be patient. Start by removing any screws or other fasteners that are visible. Then, carefully insert a plastic opening tool into the seam between the case halves and gently pry them apart. Avoid using metal tools, as these can easily scratch or damage the plastic.

Pay close attention to connectors, which are often fragile and easily broken. Use a plastic spudger to gently pry connectors loose, and avoid pulling on the wires.

Soldering with Precision: Choosing the Right Tip and Temperature

Soldering is a delicate process that requires precision and control. Choosing the right soldering iron tip and temperature is crucial for creating strong, reliable solder joints.

For general-purpose soldering, a conical tip is a good all-around choice. Chisel tips are useful for soldering larger components or surface-mount devices. Fine-point tips are ideal for soldering very small components in tight spaces.

The ideal soldering temperature depends on the type of solder being used. Lead-based solder typically melts at around 183°C (361°F), while lead-free solder requires a higher temperature, around 217°C (423°F).

Avoid overheating the solder joint, as this can damage components and weaken the connection. Apply heat to the surfaces being soldered, and then apply solder to the heated surfaces. Allow the solder to flow smoothly and form a shiny, concave joint.

Diagnosing Electrical Problems: Multimeter Mastery

The multimeter is an indispensable tool for diagnosing electrical problems in electronic devices. However, using a multimeter effectively requires understanding how to use the different settings and interpret the readings.

Before using a multimeter, always make sure it is properly set up for the measurement you are trying to make. Select the correct function (voltage, current, resistance) and range.

When measuring voltage, connect the multimeter probes in parallel with the circuit being tested. When measuring current, connect the probes in series with the circuit. When measuring resistance, disconnect the power from the circuit and connect the probes across the component being tested.

Pay close attention to the polarity of the probes. Connect the red probe to the positive terminal and the black probe to the negative terminal.

Case Study: Common Tooling Mistakes & Lessons Learned

Consider a scenario where someone is attempting to replace a smartphone battery. Using a metal pry tool instead of a plastic spudger, they scratch the delicate internal components and sever a ribbon cable. What could have been a 15-minute job now requires additional parts and technical expertise. The lesson? Always use the right tool to avoid exacerbating the problem.

Or imagine trying to desolder a surface mount capacitor with too little flux. The solder doesn't flow correctly and you apply too much heat to the component, damaging the underlying board. The lesson here is to prepare the area properly and understand the process fully before starting.

These examples highlight the importance of not just *having* the tools but understanding *how* and *when* to use them.

The Value of Experience and Continuous Learning

Ultimately, the best way to learn how to select the right tools for the job is through experience. The more you repair electronics, the better you'll become at recognizing the specific tools and techniques needed for each task.

Don't be afraid to experiment and try new things. There are many resources available online, including tutorials, forums, and videos, that can help you learn new skills and techniques.

With practice and patience, you'll develop a keen sense of how to select the right tools and techniques for any electronics repair project. It's a skill that will serve you well throughout your repair journey.

(2.5) Maintaining Your Tools: Cleaning and Care

You've invested in a good set of tools, learned how to use them effectively, and are well on your way to becoming a proficient electronics repair technician. But the journey doesn't end there. Just like any valuable asset, your tools require regular maintenance to keep them in top condition, ensuring they perform optimally, last longer, and remain safe to use. Think of this section as learning how to care for your "partners" in repair; neglecting them will only lead to headaches and increased costs down the road.

Why Tool Maintenance Matters: Beyond Just Cleanliness

Tool maintenance is more than just keeping your tools clean and organized. It's about preserving their functionality, extending their lifespan, and ensuring your safety.

- **Performance:** Clean, well-maintained tools perform better. Sharp cutting edges stay sharp, smooth-moving parts stay smooth, and accurate measuring instruments stay accurate.
- **Longevity:** Regular maintenance prevents rust, corrosion, and wear, extending the lifespan of your tools and saving you money in the long run.
- **Safety:** Clean, well-maintained tools are safer to use. Damaged or poorly maintained tools can be hazardous, leading to accidents and injuries.

Screwdrivers: Keeping the Tips Sharp and Clean

Screwdrivers are subjected to a lot of wear and tear, especially the tips. Over time, the tips can become worn, rounded, or even broken. To keep your screwdrivers in good condition, follow these tips:

- **Clean the Tips:** After each use, wipe the tips with a clean cloth to remove any dirt, grease, or debris.
- **Sharpen the Tips (Carefully):** If the tips become worn or rounded, you can sharpen them using a file or a sharpening stone. Be careful not to over-sharpen the tips, as this can make them brittle and prone to breakage. This is a task that requires patience.
- **Store Properly:** Store your screwdrivers in a tool organizer or rack to protect the tips from damage. Avoid throwing them in a drawer with other tools.

Pliers: Lubrication is Key

Pliers have moving parts that require lubrication to function smoothly. Over time, the joints can become stiff and difficult to move, making the pliers harder to use.

To keep your pliers in good condition, lubricate the joints periodically with a light oil, such as WD-40 or sewing machine oil. Apply a small amount of oil to the joints and work the pliers back and forth to distribute the lubricant. Wipe off any excess oil with a clean cloth.

Also, keep the cutting edges of your pliers sharp. If the cutting edges become dull, you can sharpen them using a file or a sharpening stone.

Soldering Iron: The Importance of Tip Maintenance

The soldering iron tip is the most critical part of the soldering station and requires regular maintenance to ensure proper heat transfer and solder flow.

- **Clean the Tip Regularly:** The soldering iron tip will oxidize over time, forming a layer of black crud that prevents the solder from flowing properly. Clean the tip regularly using a wet sponge or brass wool. Wipe the tip across the sponge or wool to remove any oxidation or debris.

- **Tin the Tip:** After cleaning the tip, tin it by applying a thin layer of solder to the tip. This will protect the tip from oxidation and improve heat transfer.
- **Avoid Overheating:** Overheating the soldering iron tip can damage it and shorten its lifespan. Use the lowest temperature setting that is necessary to melt the solder.
- **Turn it Off:** Always turn off your soldering iron when it's not in use. Leaving it on for extended periods of time can damage the tip and waste energy.

Multimeter: Battery Care and Storage

The multimeter is a precision instrument that requires proper care to ensure accurate readings.

- **Replace Batteries Regularly:** Replace the batteries as needed to ensure accurate readings. Low batteries can cause inaccurate measurements.
- **Clean the Case:** Keep the case clean and free from dirt and debris.
- **Store Properly:** Store the multimeter in a safe place to protect it from damage. Avoid dropping it or subjecting it to extreme temperatures or humidity.

Case Study: The Cost of Neglect - A Repair Technician's Tale

A seasoned electronics repair technician once shared a story about neglecting his soldering station. He rarely cleaned the tip, used excessive heat, and often left the iron on for hours. Eventually, the tip became so corroded that it was unusable, and he had to replace the entire soldering station. The cost of a few minutes of regular maintenance would have saved him hundreds of dollars. This underscores the point that a small investment in care goes a long way.

Personal Insights:

I can't emphasize enough the importance of a clean working area and a sharp mind when repairing electronics. Clutter leads to carelessness, and that can lead to mistakes or injuries. Cleaning and organizing your tools can put you in the right mindset for each repair.

Tool maintenance is not just a chore; it's an investment in your skills and your safety. By taking care of your tools, you'll ensure they perform optimally, last longer, and help you become a more proficient and successful electronics repair technician. Think of it as a ritual that prepares you for each repair, ensuring a smooth and efficient process.

Chapter 3: Understanding Electronic Components

Welcome to Chapter 3, where we'll unlock the secrets of electronic components! If tools are the instruments we use to perform repairs, then components are the very notes that make up the electronic "music" inside our devices. Understanding what these components do and how to identify them is essential for diagnosing problems and performing successful repairs.

Think of this chapter as learning the alphabet of electronics. Once you understand the basic components and their functions, you'll be able to read schematics, troubleshoot circuits, and repair devices with confidence. Don't be intimidated, we'll break it all down in a digestible way.

(3.1) Resistors, Capacitors, Inductors: Function & Identification

Imagine building a house. You need more than just walls and a roof; you need plumbing to control the flow of water, storage to hold reserves, and safety valves to prevent damage. Resistors, capacitors, and inductors are like the plumbing, storage tanks, and safety valves of electronic circuits, controlling the flow of electricity and ensuring everything works harmoniously. Understanding these three components is essential for any electronics enthusiast.

Resistors: Taming the Flow of Electrical Current

At its most basic, a resistor *resists* the flow of electrical current. Think of it like a narrow section of pipe in a water system; it restricts the flow, reducing the pressure on the other side. In an electronic circuit, resistors are used to limit current, divide voltage, and even generate heat for specific applications.

A resistor's resistance is measured in ohms (Ω). A higher resistance means the resistor will restrict the flow of current more strongly. Resistors come in various values, ranging from just a few ohms to millions of ohms. The specific value is determined by the materials used and its physical dimensions.

Identifying resistors is typically done through colored bands painted around the body. These bands follow a standard color code, where each color represents a numerical digit. Learning the color code is a valuable skill for any electronics technician. Mnemonics (memory aids) like "Better Be Right, Or Your Great Big Venture Goes Wrong" (Black, Brown, Red, Orange, Yellow, Green, Blue, Violet, Gray, White) can help you remember the order. Thankfully, many online calculators exist if you can't memorize the whole scheme.

Resistors aren't all created equal. Carbon film resistors are a common and inexpensive choice for general-purpose applications. Metal film resistors offer higher precision and better stability over temperature variations, making them suitable for more critical circuits. Wire-wound resistors are designed to handle high power levels and are often used in power supplies.

Capacitors: Storing and Releasing Electrical Energy

While resistors control the flow of current, capacitors *store* electrical energy. They're like tiny rechargeable batteries that can quickly store and release energy as needed. In an electronic circuit, capacitors are used to filter signals, smooth voltage fluctuations, and store energy for timing circuits.

A capacitor's ability to store energy is measured in farads (F), though you'll often see smaller units like microfarads (µF), nanofarads (nF), and picofarads (pF). A higher capacitance means the capacitor can store more energy.

Capacitors come in a wide variety of shapes, sizes, and materials. Ceramic capacitors are small, inexpensive, and non-polarized (meaning they can be connected in either direction). They're often used for general-purpose filtering and decoupling applications.

Electrolytic capacitors offer much higher capacitance values than ceramic capacitors but are polarized, meaning they have a positive and negative terminal that must be connected correctly. These are often used for smoothing power supply voltages.

Tantalum capacitors are also polarized and offer good performance at high frequencies. They're often used in critical circuits where stability and reliability are paramount.

Identifying capacitors can be tricky, as markings vary depending on the type and manufacturer. Capacitors are typically marked with their capacitance value and voltage rating. The voltage rating indicates the maximum voltage that the capacitor can safely handle. Exceeding the voltage rating can damage or destroy the capacitor.

Inductors: Storing Energy in a Magnetic Field

While capacitors store energy in an electric field, inductors store energy in a *magnetic* field. They're like tiny electromagnets that resist changes in current flow. In electronic circuits, inductors are used to filter signals, block high-frequency noise, and store energy in switching power supplies.

An inductor's ability to store energy is measured in henries (H), though you'll often see smaller units like microhenries (μH) and millihenries (mH). A higher inductance means the inductor can store more energy.

Inductors are typically coil-shaped, with a core made of air, iron, or ferrite. The core material affects the inductor's inductance and its performance at different frequencies.

Air-core inductors are used for high-frequency applications where low losses are important. Iron-core inductors offer higher inductance but are less efficient at high frequencies. Ferrite-core inductors offer a good balance between inductance and efficiency and are commonly used in switching power supplies.

Identifying inductors can be challenging, as markings are often cryptic or non-existent. Some inductors are marked with their inductance value, while others are marked with a code that must be looked up in a datasheet.

Working Together: The Dance of R, C, and L

Resistors, capacitors, and inductors rarely work in isolation. They often work together in circuits to create specific effects. For example, a resistor and capacitor can be combined to create a simple low-pass filter, which allows low-frequency signals to pass through while blocking high-frequency signals. An inductor and capacitor can be combined to create a resonant circuit, which oscillates at a specific frequency.

Understanding how resistors, capacitors, and inductors interact in circuits is essential for diagnosing problems and designing new electronic devices.

Mastering the fundamentals of resistors, capacitors, and inductors is a crucial step on your journey to becoming a skilled electronics repair technician.

(3.2) Diodes & Transistors: How They Work

Now that we've covered the basics of resistors, capacitors, and inductors, it's time to delve into the world of semiconductors, the materials that form the foundation of modern electronics. Diodes and transistors are two of the most fundamental semiconductor devices, acting as the switches and amplifiers that control the flow of electricity in countless electronic circuits. Understanding how these components work is key to understanding how our devices operate.

Diodes: One-Way Streets for Electrical Current

A diode, in its simplest form, is like a one-way valve for electrical current. It allows current to flow easily in one direction (forward bias) but blocks it in the opposite direction (reverse bias). This seemingly simple behavior has a wide range of applications, from converting AC voltage to DC voltage to protecting circuits from damage.

Diodes are made from semiconductor materials, typically silicon or germanium, that have been specially treated to create a *p-n junction*. This junction is the key to the diode's one-way behavior.

When a positive voltage is applied to the anode (positive terminal) and a negative voltage is applied to the cathode (negative terminal), the diode is forward biased, and current flows easily through the junction. However, when the voltage is reversed, the diode is reverse biased, and the junction blocks the flow of current.

There's always a small voltage drop across a forward-biased diode, typically around 0.6-0.7 volts for silicon diodes. This voltage drop is due to the energy required to overcome the internal resistance of the diode.

Different types of diodes are designed for specific applications. Rectifier diodes are used to convert AC voltage to DC voltage in power supplies. Zener diodes are used to regulate voltage by maintaining a constant voltage drop across them. Light-emitting diodes (LEDs) emit light when current flows through them. Schottky diodes have a lower forward voltage drop than standard diodes, making them suitable for high-speed switching applications.

The applications of diodes are vast. Rectifiers in power supplies allow our devices to be powered by the alternating current from our wall outlets by converting it to direct current. LEDs provide the light sources for displays, indicators, and lighting.

Transistors: Amplifying and Switching Electronic Signals

Transistors are the workhorses of modern electronics, acting as both amplifiers and switches. They allow a small amount of current or voltage to control a much larger current flow, enabling amplification, switching, and a wide range of other functions.

There are two main types of transistors: bipolar junction transistors (BJTs) and field-effect transistors (FETs).

- **Bipolar Junction Transistors (BJTs):** BJTs are current-controlled devices. A small current flowing into the base terminal controls a larger current flowing between the collector and emitter terminals. BJTs come in two types: NPN and PNP. In an NPN transistor, a small positive current flowing into the base turns on the larger current between collector and emitter. The opposite is true for PNP transistors.

  BJTs are commonly used in amplifiers, where a small input signal is amplified to produce a larger output signal. They are also used as switches, where a small current applied to the base turns the transistor on or off, controlling a larger current in the circuit.

- **Field-Effect Transistors (FETs):** FETs are voltage-controlled devices. A voltage applied to the gate terminal controls the current flowing between the source and drain terminals. FETs come in two main types: JFETs and MOSFETs.

MOSFETs (Metal-Oxide-Semiconductor FETs) are the most common type of FET used in modern electronics. MOSFETs are widely used in digital circuits, where they act as switches. They are also used in power amplifiers and other analog circuits.

The applications of transistors are virtually limitless. In computers, transistors act as the fundamental switches that perform logical operations. In audio amplifiers, transistors amplify the weak signals from microphones or music players.

Case Study: The Transistor Revolution: From Vacuum Tubes to Silicon Chips

The invention of the transistor in 1947 revolutionized the electronics industry. Before transistors, electronic circuits relied on bulky, power-hungry vacuum tubes. Transistors were smaller, lighter, more efficient, and more reliable than vacuum tubes.

The development of integrated circuits (ICs), which contain millions or even billions of transistors on a single silicon chip, further transformed electronics. ICs made possible the development of powerful computers, smartphones, and other electronic devices that would have been unimaginable with vacuum tubes. The transistor's impact can be seen in every modern electronic device.

Understanding how diodes and transistors work is essential for any electronics repair technician. These components are the building blocks of countless electronic circuits, and being able to troubleshoot and repair circuits containing diodes and transistors is a crucial skill.

With a solid understanding of diodes and transistors, you'll be well-equipped to tackle more advanced topics in electronics repair. You'll be able to analyze circuits, diagnose problems, and repair devices with confidence.

(3.3) Integrated Circuits (ICs): An Overview

If diodes and transistors are the individual cells in the body of electronics, integrated circuits (ICs) are the organs, each performing complex and specialized functions. They're the brains, hearts, and nervous systems of our devices, orchestrating the flow of information and controlling the actions of countless components. Understanding ICs is crucial for any aspiring electronics repair technician, even if complete IC-level repair requires specialized tools. This section provides a foundational overview.

What is an Integrated Circuit?

An integrated circuit (IC), often called a chip or microchip, is a miniature electronic circuit that has been manufactured on the surface of a thin substrate of semiconductor material. The semiconductor material used is usually silicon. Integrated circuits are used in virtually all electronic equipment today and have revolutionized the world of electronics.

ICs contain a vast number of tiny components, such as transistors, resistors, and capacitors, all interconnected to perform a specific function. These components are fabricated on a single piece of silicon using a process called photolithography, which allows for extremely precise and miniaturized circuits. This process makes circuits much smaller and cheaper than assembling them from discrete components.

The result is a highly complex circuit packed into a tiny package, offering incredible functionality in a small space. This miniaturization is what has enabled the development of powerful computers, smartphones, and other portable electronic devices.

Functionality & Versatility: The Many Faces of ICs

ICs come in a dizzying array of types, each designed for a specific purpose. Some common types include:

- **Microprocessors (CPUs):** The central processing units of computers, responsible for executing instructions and performing calculations. They are the "brains" of the computer.
- **Memory Chips (RAM, ROM):** Used to store data and instructions. RAM (Random Access Memory) provides fast, temporary storage for data that is actively being used, while ROM (Read Only Memory) stores permanent instructions that the computer needs to boot up.
- **Logic Gates:** Used to perform logical operations, such as AND, OR, and NOT. These are the fundamental building blocks of digital circuits.
- **Amplifiers:** Used to amplify weak signals, such as audio signals or radio signals.

- **Timers:** Used to generate precise time intervals.
- **Power Management ICs (PMICs):** Used to efficiently manage power distribution within a device.
- **Interface ICs:** Handle communication between different parts of a device or with external devices. Examples include USB controllers, Ethernet controllers, and display drivers.

The specific function of an IC is determined by its internal circuitry and the way it is programmed. Some ICs are designed to be programmable, allowing them to be customized for different applications.

Identifying ICs: Markings and Datasheets

ICs are typically identified by a part number printed on their surface. This part number can be used to look up the IC's datasheet, which provides detailed information about its function, pinout, electrical characteristics, and application circuits.

The pinout diagram shows the arrangement of the pins on the IC and identifies the function of each pin. This information is essential for connecting the IC to other components in a circuit.

Datasheets also provide information about the IC's electrical characteristics, such as its operating voltage, current consumption, and maximum ratings. This information is crucial for designing circuits that operate safely and reliably.

Case Study: The 555 Timer IC: A Versatile Workhorse

The 555 timer IC is one of the most popular and versatile ICs ever created. It can be used to generate a wide variety of timing signals, making it ideal for applications such as oscillators, timers, and pulse generators.

The 555 timer IC is easy to use and requires only a few external components to operate. It has been used in countless electronic projects, from simple toys to complex industrial control systems. Its enduring popularity is a testament to its versatility and reliability.

Impact and Influence

ICs have revolutionized electronics, enabling the development of smaller, faster, more powerful, and more affordable devices. They are the foundation of modern computing, communication, and control systems.

The ability to pack millions or even billions of transistors onto a single IC has led to exponential increases in computing power and has transformed the way we live, work, and interact with the world.

While complete IC-level repair is beyond the scope of this book, understanding what ICs do, how to identify them, and how to find their datasheets is an invaluable skill for any electronics repair technician. This knowledge will allow you to diagnose problems more effectively and to understand the overall function of the circuits you are working on.

(3.4) Component Testing with a Multimeter

Knowing what a component *should* do is one thing; verifying that it *actually is* doing it is another. The multimeter is your primary tool for assessing the health and functionality of electronic components. While it can't tell you everything about a component's performance, it can quickly identify common failures, such as shorts, opens, and incorrect values. This section is about transforming you from a theorist to a practical troubleshooter.

Safety First: Power Down and Discharge

Before testing any component with a multimeter, it is absolutely essential to disconnect the power from the circuit. Never attempt to measure voltage or resistance on a live circuit unless you are properly trained and understand the risks involved.

Capacitors can store a significant amount of electrical energy, even after the power has been disconnected. Before testing any component in a circuit containing capacitors, discharge the capacitors by shorting their terminals with a resistor. Use an insulated tool to do this, and be careful not to touch the bare leads of the resistor.

Resistors: Verifying the Value

Testing a resistor with a multimeter is straightforward. Simply set the multimeter to the ohms (Ω) setting and connect the probes to the resistor's leads. The multimeter will display the resistance value.

The measured value should be close to the value indicated by the color code. Resistors have a tolerance, typically 5% or 10%, meaning the actual resistance value can vary by that percentage from the nominal value.

If the measured resistance is significantly different from the expected value, or if the multimeter displays "OL" (overload) or a very low resistance (close to zero), the resistor is likely faulty and needs to be replaced.

It's important to note that when measuring resistors *in-circuit,* other components in the circuit can affect the reading. For accurate measurements, it's best to test resistors out of circuit.

Capacitors: Checking for Shorts and Opens

Multimeters are not ideal for precisely measuring capacitance, as they often lack the necessary accuracy. However, they can be used to check for common capacitor failures, such as shorts and opens.

To check for a shorted capacitor, set the multimeter to the ohms (Ω) setting and connect the probes to the capacitor's leads. A good capacitor should show a high resistance (approaching infinity). If the multimeter displays a very low resistance (close to zero), the capacitor is likely shorted and needs to be replaced.

To check for an open capacitor, set the multimeter to the continuity setting. A good capacitor should not conduct electricity. If the multimeter beeps, indicating continuity, the capacitor is likely faulty.

Some multimeters have a capacitance setting that can be used to measure the capacitance value. However, this setting is often not very accurate, especially for small capacitors. A dedicated capacitance meter provides more accurate measurements.

Diodes: Confirming One-Way Behavior

Diodes are designed to allow current to flow in one direction only. A multimeter can be used to verify this behavior.

Set the multimeter to the diode testing setting. Connect the red probe (positive) to the anode (positive terminal) and the black probe (negative) to the cathode (negative terminal). The multimeter should display a voltage drop of around 0.6-0.7 volts for silicon diodes.

Now, reverse the probes. Connect the red probe to the cathode and the black probe to the anode. The multimeter should display "OL" (overload) or a very high resistance, indicating that the diode is blocking the flow of current.

If the diode shows a low resistance in both directions, it is likely shorted. If it shows a high resistance in both directions, it is likely open. In either case, the diode needs to be replaced.

Transistors: A More Complex Task

Testing transistors with a multimeter is more complex than testing resistors, capacitors, or diodes. A multimeter can be used to check for shorts or opens between the transistor's terminals, but it cannot fully verify the transistor's performance.

To test a BJT (bipolar junction transistor), you can use the diode testing setting to check the p-n junctions between the base and collector, and between the base and emitter. Each junction should behave like a diode, showing a voltage drop of around 0.6-0.7 volts in one direction and blocking current in the opposite direction.

To test a MOSFET (metal-oxide-semiconductor field-effect transistor), you can use the ohms (Ω) setting to check for shorts between the gate and the source, gate and the drain, and source and drain. There should be no continuity between any of these terminals.

A transistor tester is a more specialized tool that can be used to fully verify the transistor's performance, including its gain, saturation voltage, and switching speed.

Case Study: The Intermittent Resistor

A repair technician was troubleshooting a malfunctioning power supply. The multimeter showed that the main series resistor was within tolerance. However, the circuit was malfunctioning under full load. After flexing the resistor leads, the technician noticed that the multimeter reading was now showing an open circuit. The resistor only failed under stress, which is a common occurrence.

This case illustrates the importance of not just measuring components but also checking for other potential problems, such as loose connections or intermittent failures.

Component testing with a multimeter is a valuable skill for any electronics repair technician. It allows you to quickly identify common component failures and narrow down the source of a problem.

(3.5) Reading Component Markings and Datasheets

Successfully identifying a component and testing it are important, but fully understanding its capabilities and limitations requires deciphering the markings on the component itself and consulting its datasheet. Think of component markings as the component's name tag and the datasheet as its resume, revealing its skills, experience, and potential pitfalls. This skill is important for technicians that do component-level repair.

Component Markings: Deciphering the Code

Electronic components are often marked with a combination of letters and numbers that provide information about their value, tolerance, voltage rating, and other characteristics. These markings can seem cryptic at first, but with a little practice, you can learn to decipher them.

- **Resistor Color Codes:** As discussed earlier, resistors use colored bands to indicate their resistance value. Learning the resistor color code is an essential skill for any electronics technician. Many online tools can assist in decoding these bands.
- **Capacitor Markings:** Capacitors are typically marked with their capacitance value in picofarads (pF), nanofarads (nF), or microfarads (µF), as well as their voltage rating. Some capacitors also have a tolerance code, indicating the range of possible capacitance values.
- **Diode Markings:** Diodes are typically marked with a part number that identifies their type and characteristics. The part number can be used to look up the diode's datasheet.
- **Transistor Markings:** Transistors are also typically marked with a part number that identifies their type and characteristics. The part number can be used to look up the transistor's datasheet.

- **IC Markings:** Integrated circuits have the most complex markings, as they require much more information. Always use the part number for the particular IC.

It's important to note that component markings can vary depending on the manufacturer and the type of component. Some components may have more detailed markings than others.

Datasheets: The Component's Resume

A datasheet is a technical document that provides detailed information about an electronic component. It includes information about the component's electrical characteristics, pinout, application circuits, and other important specifications.

Datasheets are essential for understanding how a component works and how to use it properly. They are also invaluable for troubleshooting circuits and identifying potential problems.

Datasheets can typically be found online on the manufacturer's website or on component database websites like AllDataSheet or Octopart. Simply search for the component's part number to find its datasheet.

Key Information Found in Datasheets:

- **Pinout Diagram:** Shows the arrangement of the pins on the component and identifies the function of each pin.
- **Electrical Characteristics:** Specifies the component's operating voltage, current consumption, input and output impedance, and other electrical parameters.
- **Maximum Ratings:** Specifies the maximum voltage, current, power, and temperature that the component can safely handle. Exceeding these ratings can damage or destroy the component.
- **Application Circuits:** Provides example circuits showing how to use the component in a typical application.
- **Package Information:** Specifies the physical dimensions and mounting information for the component.

Understanding how to read and interpret datasheets is an essential skill for any electronics repair technician. It allows you to fully understand the capabilities and limitations of a component and to use it effectively in your designs and repairs.

Case Study: Datasheet Saves the Day – Troubleshooting a Power Supply

A technician was troubleshooting a malfunctioning power supply. The power supply was producing the correct output voltage, but it was overheating. The technician suspected that one of the components in the power supply was drawing too much current.

Using the power supply's schematic, the technician identified a voltage regulator IC. He then looked up the datasheet for the IC and found that its maximum current rating was 1 amp. Using a multimeter, the technician measured the current flowing through the IC and found that it was 1.2 amps, exceeding its maximum rating.

The technician replaced the voltage regulator IC with a new one that had a higher current rating, and the power supply stopped overheating. The datasheet was essential for identifying the problem and finding a solution.

In short, successfully making use of datasheets can be the different between successfully repairing an IC.

Reading component markings and datasheets can seem daunting at first, but with practice, it becomes a valuable skill that will greatly enhance your ability to troubleshoot and repair electronic devices. Just remember that there are a wealth of free resources online and that mastering electronics repair takes time.

Chapter 4: Soldering and Desoldering Fundamentals

(Image Suggestion: A split image. One side shows a perfectly soldered joint - shiny and smooth. The other side shows a poorly soldered joint - dull, cracked, and blob-like.)

Welcome to Chapter 4, where we'll delve into the art and science of soldering and desoldering! If understanding components is like knowing the notes on a musical score, then soldering and desoldering are the techniques for playing those notes and creating beautiful electronic circuits.

Mastering these skills is essential for any electronics repair technician. Soldering allows you to create permanent electrical connections, while desoldering allows you to safely remove components for replacement or repair. This chapter will walk you through the process, step by step, equipping you with the knowledge and practice tips you'll need to succeed.

(4.1) Preparing for Soldering: Safety First

Soldering, at its core, involves melting metal with a hot iron to fuse electronic components together. While the results can be rewarding – a repaired device, a functional circuit – the process itself presents several potential hazards that must be taken seriously. Approaching soldering with a healthy respect for safety isn't just a good idea; it's crucial for your well-being and the longevity of your repair hobby or career. Before you even plug in that soldering iron, it's time for a safety check.

The Silent Threat: Solder Fumes

One of the most insidious dangers of soldering is the inhalation of solder fumes. These fumes are released when the flux in the solder is heated, and they contain a variety of potentially harmful substances, including:

- **Rosin:** Rosin is a natural resin used as a fluxing agent in many solders. When heated, it releases airborne particles that can irritate the lungs and respiratory system. Prolonged exposure can lead to asthma, bronchitis, and other respiratory problems.

- **Lead (in Lead-Based Solder):** Lead is a neurotoxin that can damage the brain and nervous system. While lead-free solders are becoming more common, many solders still contain lead. Inhaling lead fumes or ingesting lead can lead to lead poisoning, which can have serious health consequences.
- **Other Metals:** Solder fumes may also contain small amounts of other metals, such as tin, copper, and silver, which can also be harmful to the respiratory system.

The key to minimizing the risk of inhaling solder fumes is proper ventilation. Always work in a well-ventilated area. Open a window and use a fan to blow the fumes away from your face. A fume extractor is an even better solution, as it actively draws the fumes away from your work area and filters out the harmful particles.

Even if you're using lead-free solder, it's still important to avoid inhaling the fumes, as they can still irritate your lungs.

Burn Hazards: Respecting the Heat

The soldering iron tip can reach temperatures of up to 450°C (842°F), hot enough to cause severe burns in a fraction of a second. Molten solder can also splatter and cause burns.

To protect yourself from burns, take the following precautions:

- **Never Touch the Soldering Iron Tip:** Always assume the soldering iron tip is hot, even if it doesn't look like it.
- **Use a Soldering Iron Stand:** When not in use, always place the soldering iron in a stand to prevent it from accidentally touching anything.
- **Wear Protective Clothing:** Wear long sleeves and closed-toe shoes to protect your skin from burns.
- **Use Heat-Resistant Gloves or Finger Cots:** Consider wearing heat-resistant gloves or finger cots to protect your hands from accidental contact with the soldering iron tip or molten solder.
- **Be Careful with Molten Solder:** Be careful not to splatter molten solder. If you do accidentally get molten solder on your skin, immediately rinse the burn with cool water.

Electrical Hazards: Avoiding Shocks

Soldering involves working with electricity, and there is always a risk of electrical shock. To minimize the risk of electrical shock, take the following precautions:

- **Disconnect the Power:** Always disconnect the power from the circuit before soldering or desoldering components.
- **Use Insulated Tools:** Use insulated tools to prevent accidental contact with live circuits.
- **Work on a Dry Surface:** Avoid working on a wet surface, as water can conduct electricity.
- **Be Aware of Static Electricity:** Static electricity can damage sensitive electronic components. Use an anti-static wrist strap to discharge any static electricity before working on electronic devices.

Case Study: The Fume Extractor That Saved a Career

A seasoned electronics technician had been soldering for years without using a fume extractor. He developed a persistent cough and shortness of breath. His doctor diagnosed him with asthma and warned him that his soldering could be contributing to his condition.

The technician invested in a fume extractor and immediately noticed a difference. His cough subsided, and his breathing improved. He realized that he had been unknowingly damaging his lungs for years by inhaling solder fumes. He now emphasizes the importance of using a fume extractor to all of his colleagues.

Prioritizing safety when soldering is not just about protecting yourself from immediate harm; it's about protecting your long-term health and well-being. By taking the necessary precautions, you can enjoy the rewarding experience of electronics repair without putting yourself at risk. Remember to stay focused while soldering. Take breaks when you need them to avoid making dangerous mistakes.

(4.2) Through-Hole Soldering: A Step-by-Step Guide

Through-hole soldering is a fundamental technique in electronics, forming the backbone of many circuit boards. It involves inserting component leads through pre-drilled holes in the board and then soldering those leads to the surrounding copper pads. While surface-mount technology dominates modern electronics, through-hole soldering remains relevant for certain components, hobbyist projects, and repair work. Think of mastering through-hole soldering as building a solid foundation before moving on to more complex techniques.

The Importance of Preparation: Cleanliness and Stability

Before you even heat up your soldering iron, proper preparation is key to achieving a good solder joint. This involves both cleaning the components and ensuring they are stable during the process.

First, clean the component leads and the circuit board pads with isopropyl alcohol. This removes any dirt, grease, or oxidation that can interfere with the soldering process, preventing the solder from flowing smoothly and creating a strong bond. A cotton swab or a small brush can be used to scrub the surfaces.

Next, insert the component leads through the holes in the circuit board. Bending the leads slightly on the underside of the board can help hold the component in place while you solder. This is especially important for components with only two leads, such as resistors and diodes. For larger components, you may need to use a clamp or other support to keep them from moving. You can also purchase heat-resistant tape.

The goal is to have a clean and stable connection before you even apply heat. This sets the stage for a successful and reliable solder joint.

The Dance of Heat and Solder: Creating the Bond

Now for the soldering itself, which can be described as a "dance" between heat and solder. The goal is to heat both the component lead and the copper pad simultaneously and then apply the solder to create a molten bridge between the two.

Start by touching the soldering iron tip to both the component lead and the circuit board pad simultaneously. The iron should be clean and tinned with a small amount of solder. Apply heat for a few seconds, until both the lead and the pad are hot enough to melt the solder. The amount of time required will depend on the size of the components and the power of your soldering iron.

Next, touch the solder to the heated pad and lead. The solder should melt and flow smoothly around the lead and onto the pad. Use just enough solder to create a solid connection, but avoid using too much, as this can create a solder bridge (more on that later).

Remove the solder first, then remove the soldering iron. This prevents the solder joint from being disturbed while it cools. Hold the circuit board still for a few seconds until the solder has solidified.

A good solder joint should be shiny, smooth, and concave. It should have a good "wetting" angle, meaning the solder should flow smoothly onto the pad and lead, creating a seamless connection.

Trimming the Leads: Finishing the Job

Once the solder joint has cooled completely, trim the excess component leads with wire cutters. Cut the leads as close to the solder joint as possible, but be careful not to damage the solder joint in the process.

A clean trim not only improves the appearance of the circuit board but also prevents the leads from accidentally shorting to other components.

Common Pitfalls and How to Avoid Them

Through-hole soldering is relatively straightforward, but there are a few common pitfalls to watch out for:

- **Cold Solder Joints:** As mentioned previously, cold solder joints are weak and unreliable connections caused by insufficient heat. They typically look dull and grainy. To avoid cold solder joints, make sure to heat both the component lead and the circuit board pad thoroughly before applying the solder.
- **Solder Bridges:** Solder bridges are unwanted connections between two adjacent pads or leads. They are typically caused by using too much solder or by not controlling the flow of solder properly. To avoid solder bridges, use only the amount of solder needed and clean the iron tip frequently.
- **Overheating:** Overheating components can damage them and shorten their lifespan. To avoid overheating, use the lowest

temperature setting that is necessary to melt the solder and avoid leaving the soldering iron on the component for too long.

Case Study: The Importance of a Good Solder Joint – A Robotic Arm Fails

An engineering student was working on a robotic arm project. The arm was controlled by a microcontroller that was connected to several motors. The student carefully soldered all the components together, but the arm kept malfunctioning.

After some troubleshooting, the student discovered that one of the solder joints on the microcontroller was a cold solder joint. The joint was making intermittent contact, causing the microcontroller to malfunction. The student resoldered the joint properly, and the robotic arm started working perfectly.

This case illustrates the importance of creating good solder joints for reliable circuit operation.

With practice and attention to detail, you can master through-hole soldering and create strong, reliable connections that will last for years to come. This technique forms a cornerstone of your electronics repair skills, opening doors to countless projects and repairs.

(4.3) Surface Mount Soldering (SMD): Techniques & Tips

Welcome to the world of surface mount soldering! If through-hole soldering is like building with Lego bricks, then surface mount soldering is like building with micro-Lego bricks. Surface Mount Devices (SMDs) are the tiny components that populate most modern circuit boards. They're smaller, lighter, and more densely packed than through-hole components, enabling the miniaturization of electronic devices.

While SMD soldering can seem daunting at first, with the right tools, techniques, and a bit of patience, it can be mastered. This section aims to demystify the process, providing you with a practical guide to successfully soldering SMDs and unlocking a new level of repair and modification capabilities. Mastering this technique lets you repair devices that you otherwise would not be able to.

The Right Tools for the Job: Magnification and Precision

SMD soldering requires specialized tools to handle the tiny components and create precise solder joints. Here are some essential tools to have in your arsenal:

- **Magnification:** Magnification is essential for seeing the tiny components and solder joints clearly. A magnifying glass, a microscope, or a head-mounted magnifier can be used.
- **Fine-Tip Soldering Iron:** A soldering iron with a fine tip is necessary for applying heat precisely to the small pads and leads of SMDs. Adjustable temperature control is also crucial.
- **Tweezers:** Fine-tipped tweezers are essential for picking up and placing SMDs.
- **Solder Paste:** Solder paste is a mixture of solder particles and flux, used to create solder joints.
- **Solder Wick:** Solder wick is a braided copper wire used to remove excess solder.
- **Hot Air Rework Station (Optional but Recommended):** A hot air rework station is a specialized tool that blows hot air onto the circuit board, melting the solder and allowing you to remove or replace SMDs. This tool is used in many professional applications.
- **Flux:** Liquid flux or a flux pen can help improve solder flow and create stronger solder joints.

Applying Solder Paste: The Key to Even Connections

Applying solder paste correctly is crucial for successful SMD soldering. The goal is to apply a small, even amount of solder paste to each pad on the circuit board. There are several ways to apply solder paste:

- **Syringe:** A syringe with a fine needle can be used to apply a precise amount of solder paste to each pad.
- **Solder Paste Dispenser:** A solder paste dispenser is a specialized tool that dispenses a controlled amount of solder paste.
- **Stencil:** A stencil is a thin sheet of metal or plastic with holes that match the pads on the circuit board. The stencil is placed over the circuit board, and solder paste is applied using a squeegee.

The amount of solder paste needed will depend on the size of the pad and the type of component being soldered. Use just enough solder paste to cover the pad, but avoid using too much, as this can cause solder bridges.

Placing the Components: A Steady Hand and a Keen Eye

Placing the components accurately onto the solder paste is another crucial step in SMD soldering. Use fine-tipped tweezers to pick up the component and carefully place it onto the pads. Make sure the component is aligned correctly and that all the pins are in contact with the solder paste.

A steady hand and good eyesight are essential for this step. If you have trouble seeing the small components, use magnification.

Reflowing the Solder: Melting the Bond

Once the components are placed, the solder paste needs to be reflowed, meaning it needs to be heated until it melts and creates a solder joint between the component and the circuit board. There are several ways to reflow solder paste:

- **Soldering Iron:** A fine-tipped soldering iron can be used to reflow solder paste on small components. Touch the soldering iron tip to the pad next to the component lead, then apply a small amount of solder to the lead itself.
- **Hot Air Rework Station:** A hot air rework station is the preferred method for reflowing solder paste on larger components or multiple components at once. Heat the component from above using a circular motion until the solder paste melts and the component settles into place.
- **Reflow Oven:** A reflow oven is a specialized oven that is used to reflow solder paste on entire circuit boards. Reflow ovens provide precise temperature control and are ideal for mass production.

Be careful not to overheat the components, as this can damage them. Use the lowest temperature setting that is necessary to melt the solder paste.

Inspecting the Joint: Quality Control

After reflowing the solder, inspect the solder joint with a magnifying glass or microscope to ensure it is properly formed and free of defects. A good solder joint should be shiny, smooth, and have a good "wetting" angle. Look for the following defects:

- **Solder Bridges:** Unwanted connections between two adjacent pads or leads.
- **Cold Solder Joints:** Dull and grainy solder joints caused by insufficient heat.
- **Insufficient Solder:** Too little solder, resulting in a weak connection.
- **Tombstoning:** A component standing on one end, with the other end not soldered.

Case Study: Resurrecting a Graphics Card with Hot Air

A computer enthusiast had a high-end graphics card that had stopped working. After doing some research, he suspected that one of the surface-mount components on the card had come loose.

Using a hot air rework station, he carefully reflowed the solder on the suspected component. After the component cooled, the graphics card started working perfectly again. He avoided buying an entirely new card by successfully repairing the old one.

Surface mount soldering is a challenging but rewarding skill. With practice and the right tools, you can master this technique and unlock a new level of capabilities in electronics repair and modification.

(4.4) Desoldering Techniques: Wick, Pump, and Hot Air

Just as soldering allows you to build circuits, desoldering allows you to dismantle them, either to replace a faulty component or to salvage parts from a discarded device. Mastering desoldering is crucial for repair, modification, and reverse engineering. While soldering is an additive process, desoldering is subtractive, requiring careful technique to avoid damaging components or the circuit board. Think of these techniques as your tools for safely "undoing" what soldering has done.

The Solder Wick: Absorbing Solder Like a Sponge

Solder wick, also known as desoldering braid, is a simple but effective tool for removing solder from through-hole and surface-mount components. It consists of a braided copper wire that acts like a sponge, absorbing molten solder through capillary action.

To use solder wick, place it on top of the solder joint and heat it with a soldering iron. The solder will melt and be drawn into the wick. Once the wick is saturated with solder, remove it and cut off the used portion.

Solder wick is best suited for removing small amounts of solder, such as those found on individual through-hole component leads or small surface-mount pads. It is not as effective for removing large amounts of solder or for desoldering multi-pin components.

The effectiveness of solder wick depends on the quality of the wick and the temperature of the soldering iron. Use a high-quality solder wick that is pre-treated with flux. Set the soldering iron to a temperature that is hot enough to melt the solder quickly but not so hot that it damages the components or circuit board. Also, always add new flux to the area you're working on, or even to the wick itself.

The Desoldering Pump: Sucking Solder Away

A desoldering pump, also known as a solder sucker, is a spring-loaded device that creates a vacuum to suck up molten solder. It is a more powerful desoldering tool than solder wick and is better suited for removing larger amounts of solder.

To use a desoldering pump, first, heat the solder joint with a soldering iron. Once the solder is molten, quickly position the desoldering pump tip over the solder joint and press the trigger. The spring-loaded plunger will create a vacuum that sucks up the solder.

Desoldering pumps come in two main types: plunger-style and bulb-style. Plunger-style desoldering pumps are more powerful and are better suited for removing large amounts of solder. Bulb-style desoldering pumps are smaller and easier to use in tight spaces.

The effectiveness of a desoldering pump depends on the cleanliness of the tip and the speed of the plunger. Clean the tip of the desoldering pump regularly to remove any accumulated solder. Make sure the plunger moves quickly and smoothly to create a strong vacuum. Also, it's important to apply heat directly to the pin or component you're trying to desolder, or it won't work.

Hot Air Rework: A Powerful Technique for SMDs

Hot air rework stations provide a controlled stream of hot air, making them ideal for desoldering surface-mount components (SMDs). The hot air melts all the solder joints simultaneously, allowing you to lift the component off the board without damaging it.

To use a hot air rework station, first, apply a small amount of flux to the component and the surrounding pads. Then, select the appropriate nozzle for the component size. Position the nozzle over the component and turn on the hot air.

Move the nozzle in a circular motion to evenly heat the component and the surrounding pads. Watch the solder carefully. Once the solder is molten, gently lift the component off the board using tweezers.

Hot air rework requires practice and patience. Be careful not to overheat the components or circuit board, as this can damage them. Use the lowest temperature and airflow settings that are necessary to melt the solder.

Case Study: Saving a Vintage Amplifier with Desoldering Skills

A vintage audio enthusiast had a prized amplifier that had stopped working. After troubleshooting the circuit, he discovered that one of the transistors had failed. However, the transistor was soldered directly to the circuit board, making it difficult to remove without damaging the board.

Using a combination of solder wick and a desoldering pump, he carefully removed the solder from the transistor leads. He then replaced the transistor with a new one, and the amplifier started working perfectly again. His desoldering skills allowed him to save a valuable piece of audio equipment from the landfill.

Mastering desoldering techniques is an essential skill for any electronics repair technician. Whether you're using solder wick, a desoldering pump, or a hot air rework station, the key is to use the right tool for the job and to exercise caution and patience. With practice, you can safely and effectively remove components from circuit boards, opening the door to countless repair and modification opportunities.

(4.5) Troubleshooting Soldering Issues: Common Mistakes

Even with careful preparation and meticulous technique, soldering mistakes can happen. The good news is that most soldering issues are easily identifiable and correctable. This section is designed to be your troubleshooting guide, helping you diagnose common soldering defects, understand their root causes, and implement effective solutions to ensure reliable connections. Learning to spot and fix these errors is just as important as learning to solder correctly in the first place.

The Cold Solder Joint: A Weak and Unreliable Connection

The cold solder joint is perhaps the most common and troublesome soldering defect. It's characterized by a dull, grainy appearance and a lack of proper wetting, meaning the solder hasn't flowed smoothly onto the pad and lead. Cold solder joints are weak, unreliable, and can cause intermittent circuit failures.

The root cause of a cold solder joint is insufficient heat. Either the soldering iron wasn't hot enough, or the heat wasn't applied for long enough to properly melt the solder and create a strong bond. Other causes include a dirty iron tip or oxidized components.

To correct a cold solder joint, first, clean the joint with isopropyl alcohol to remove any dirt or flux residue. Then, apply fresh flux to the joint and reheat it with the soldering iron. Make sure to heat both the lead and the pad simultaneously. Apply more solder if necessary, and allow the joint to cool completely before moving the circuit board.

A properly resoldered joint should be shiny, smooth, and concave, with a good wetting angle.

The Solder Bridge: An Unwanted Connection

A solder bridge is an unintended connection between two adjacent pads or leads. Solder bridges can cause short circuits and prevent circuits from functioning properly.

Solder bridges are typically caused by using too much solder or by not controlling the flow of solder properly. They can also be caused by dirty iron tips or oxidized components.

To remove a solder bridge, first, clean the area with isopropyl alcohol. Then, use solder wick or a desoldering pump to remove the excess solder. If the solder bridge is small, you may be able to simply drag the soldering iron tip across it to break the connection.

Be careful not to damage the pads or leads while removing a solder bridge. Use a low-temperature setting on your soldering iron and avoid applying excessive force.

Insufficient Solder: A Starved Connection

Insufficient solder results in a weak and incomplete connection. The solder joint may look thin and patchy, and the component may not be securely attached to the circuit board.

Insufficient solder is typically caused by not applying enough solder during the soldering process or by using a solder with too little flux.

To correct a joint with insufficient solder, first, clean the joint with isopropyl alcohol. Then, apply fresh flux to the joint and reheat it with the soldering iron. Apply more solder until the joint is properly formed.

Make sure to use a solder with a sufficient amount of flux to ensure proper wetting.

Excessive Solder: A Blobby Mess

While not as problematic as a cold solder joint, excessive solder can still cause problems. It can make it difficult to inspect the joint, and it can increase the risk of solder bridges.

Excessive solder is typically caused by applying too much solder during the soldering process or by using a solder with too much flux.

To remove excessive solder, use solder wick or a desoldering pump to remove the excess solder. Be careful not to overheat the joint while removing the solder.

Damaged Pads: A Tragic Outcome

Overheating or using excessive force can damage the pads on a circuit board, making it difficult to solder components. Damaged pads may lift off the board, crack, or become detached from the underlying copper traces.

Preventing damaged pads is much easier than repairing them. Use the lowest temperature setting that is necessary to melt the solder, avoid applying excessive force, and work carefully to avoid damaging the pads.

If a pad is slightly lifted, you may be able to carefully press it back down onto the board and resolder it. If a pad is severely damaged or detached, you may need to repair it by creating a jumper wire to connect the component to the underlying trace.

Case Study: The Mysterious Intermittent Failure

An electronics enthusiast was repairing a vintage synthesizer. The synthesizer would work for a few minutes, then suddenly stop working. After some troubleshooting, he discovered that one of the resistors had a cold solder joint.

The cold solder joint was making intermittent contact, causing the synthesizer to malfunction. The enthusiast resoldered the joint properly, and the synthesizer started working reliably. This case illustrates how even a single cold solder joint can cause significant problems.

Troubleshooting soldering issues is a valuable skill that will save you time, money, and frustration. By learning to identify common soldering defects, understand their root causes, and implement effective solutions, you can ensure that your solder joints are strong, reliable, and long-lasting.

Part II: Troubleshooting & Repairing Common Devices

Chapter 5: Mastering Troubleshooting Techniques

Welcome to Chapter 5, where we'll transition from simply understanding components to becoming skilled troubleshooters! Repairing electronics isn't just about replacing broken parts; it's about figuring out *why* they broke in the first place and identifying the root cause of the problem. Think of this chapter as learning to become a detective, piecing together clues to solve the mystery of the malfunctioning device.

While it may seem daunting, troubleshooting is a skill that can be learned and honed with practice. This chapter will provide you with a systematic approach to diagnosis, along with the techniques and knowledge you need to become a confident and effective troubleshooter.

(5.1) A Systematic Approach to Diagnosis

Troubleshooting electronics is a skill that's part art and part science. While intuition and experience certainly play a role, relying solely on guesswork can lead to wasted time, frustration, and even further damage to the device you're trying to repair. This is where a systematic approach comes in. A structured diagnostic process transforms troubleshooting from a chaotic hunt-and-peck exercise into a methodical investigation, maximizing your chances of success. Think of it like following a map instead of wandering aimlessly in the woods.

Beyond the Guesswork: A Foundation for Success

A systematic approach to diagnosis isn't just about following a rigid set of steps; it's about developing a mindset of logical thinking and problem-solving. It's about asking the right questions, gathering the right data, and testing your assumptions in a controlled and organized manner. By embracing this approach, you'll not only become a more effective troubleshooter but also gain a deeper understanding of how electronic circuits work.

Step 1: The Information Gathering Phase - Become an Expert on the Failure

The first step in any troubleshooting process is to gather as much information as possible about the problem. Think of yourself as a detective collecting clues at a crime scene. The more information you have, the easier it will be to identify the culprit.

Start by asking yourself (or the owner of the device) the following questions:

- **What is the device supposed to do?** Understanding the device's intended function is crucial for identifying what is not working correctly.
- **What is the device doing (or not doing) instead?** Describe the symptoms in as much detail as possible. Be specific about what is working and what is not working.
- **When did the problem start?** Knowing when the problem started can provide valuable clues about the cause. Was it sudden or gradual?
- **What were the circumstances surrounding the failure?** Was the device dropped, exposed to moisture, or subjected to a power surge? Any unusual events leading up to the failure can provide valuable insights.
- **What has already been tried?** Knowing what steps have already been taken can prevent you from wasting time on things that have already been ruled out.

This initial information gathering phase is critical. Never underestimate the power of a detailed history.

Step 2: Defining the Problem with Precision

Once you've gathered as much information as possible, it's time to define the problem in specific terms. Avoid vague descriptions like "The device doesn't work." Instead, aim for a precise and detailed statement of the symptoms.

For example, instead of saying "The TV doesn't work," say "The TV turns on, but there is no picture, and the screen is completely black. The power light is on, but there is no sound."

A precise definition of the problem will help you focus your troubleshooting efforts and avoid wasting time on irrelevant areas.

Step 3: Formulating Hypotheses - Educated Guesswork

With a clear definition of the problem in hand, it's time to formulate a list of possible causes. These are your hypotheses – educated guesses about what might be causing the problem.

Start by considering the most likely causes, based on the information you've gathered. For example, if the device is completely dead, a power supply failure is a likely suspect. If the device turns on but has no display, a problem with the display panel or its associated circuitry is a possibility. If a certain function isn't working, try to look for the components related to that.

List your hypotheses in order of likelihood, starting with the most probable and working your way down to the less likely. This will help you prioritize your testing efforts.

Step 4: Testing Your Hypotheses - Gathering Evidence

Now comes the scientific part – testing your hypotheses one by one to gather evidence that either supports or refutes them. This is where your multimeter, visual inspection skills, and other tools come into play.

Start with the easiest and most accessible tests. For example, check the power supply voltage with a multimeter. If the voltage is incorrect, you've likely found the cause of the problem. If the voltage is correct, move on to the next hypothesis.

As you perform your tests, keep careful notes of your findings. This will help you keep track of what you've already tested and what you still need to test.

Step 5: Analyzing the Results - Truth or False?

After each test, analyze the results to determine whether they support or refute your hypothesis. If the results support your hypothesis, you may have found the cause of the problem. However, it's important to confirm your findings with additional tests.

If the results refute your hypothesis, cross it off your list and move on to the next one. Don't be afraid to revise your hypotheses as you gather more information.

Step 6: Isolating the Fault - Zeroing In

Once you've identified the most likely cause of the problem, it's time to isolate the faulty component or circuit. This may involve removing components from the circuit and testing them separately.

For example, if you suspect that a resistor is faulty, remove it from the circuit and measure its resistance with a multimeter. If the resistance is significantly different from the expected value, you've likely found the culprit.

Step 7: Repair or Replace - The Fix

After isolating the fault, it's time to repair or replace the faulty component or circuit. If the component is easily replaceable, such as a resistor or capacitor, simply replace it with a new one. If the circuit is more complex, you may need to repair it by soldering broken connections or replacing damaged traces.

Step 8: Testing and Verification - The Final Check

After making the repair, it's crucial to test the device to verify that the problem has been resolved. Turn on the device and check that all functions are working correctly. If the problem persists, you may need to revisit your hypotheses and continue troubleshooting.

A systematic approach to diagnosis is a powerful tool that can help you troubleshoot even the most complex electronic problems. By following these steps, you can transform from a frustrated guesser into a confident and effective troubleshooter.

(5.2) Visual Inspection: Identifying Obvious Problems

In the realm of electronics troubleshooting, it's easy to get caught up in complex measurements and intricate circuit analysis. However, one of the most effective and often overlooked techniques is a simple visual inspection. Training your eyes to spot obvious problems can save you hours of frustration and quickly lead you to the source of the malfunction. Think of visual inspection as the first line of defense, a quick and noninvasive way to identify potential issues before diving into more complex diagnostic procedures. This skill is highly rewarding.

More Than Just a Glance: The Art of Seeing

Visual inspection is more than just a cursory glance at the circuit board or device. It's an active process of observation, looking for telltale signs of damage, wear, or malfunction. It requires a keen eye, attention to detail, and a knowledge of what to look for. It's about training your eye to see what others might miss.

Often the most obvious is overlooked by inexperienced technicians, this is why even the most experienced technician still perform visual inspections.

The Essential Tools: Light and Magnification

To perform an effective visual inspection, you'll need two essential tools:

- **Bright Light Source:** A bright light source is crucial for illuminating the circuit board and revealing subtle details. A desk lamp with a flexible arm or a flashlight can be used.
- **Magnification:** Magnification allows you to get a closer look at the components and connections. A magnifying glass, a microscope, or a head-mounted magnifier can be used.

With these two tools in hand, you're ready to start your visual inspection.

Key Areas to Examine: A Checklist for the Eye

As you visually inspect the device, pay close attention to the following areas:

- **Components:** Look for components that are burned, cracked, discolored, or otherwise damaged. Resistors that have overheated may have a charred or discolored appearance. Capacitors that have failed may be swollen, bulged, or leaking electrolyte. Integrated circuits (ICs) that have been damaged may have cracked cases or burned pins.
- **Solder Joints:** Look for solder joints that are cracked, dull, grainy, or otherwise poorly formed. Cold solder joints, as discussed earlier, are a common cause of problems. Also, look for solder bridges, which are unwanted connections between two adjacent pads or leads.

- **Circuit Board:** Look for cracks, breaks, or other damage to the circuit board. Also, look for signs of corrosion, especially around battery terminals or in areas that may have been exposed to moisture.
- **Connectors:** Look for loose, broken, or corroded connectors. Make sure that all connectors are properly seated and that there are no broken wires or pins.
- **Wiring:** Look for frayed, cracked, or broken wires. Make sure that all wires are properly connected and that there are no shorts or open circuits.
- **Power Supply:** Inspect the power supply for any signs of damage, such as blown fuses, burned components, or leaking capacitors. Power supplies are a common point of failure in electronic devices.
- **Check for Foreign Objects:** It is not uncommon to find a loose screw, metal shard, or other debris shorting traces and/or components.
- **Look for Signs of Tampering:** Check for loose screws, missing labels, or any other indication that someone else has been inside the device.

These visual cues can often point you directly to the source of the problem, saving you valuable troubleshooting time.

The Sense of Smell: An Unexpected Tool

While visual inspection is primarily a visual process, your sense of smell can also be a valuable tool. A burning smell can often indicate an overheated or shorted component. A fishy smell can indicate a leaking capacitor. If you detect any unusual odors, investigate further.

Case Study: The Swollen Capacitor That Saved Hours of Troubleshooting

A computer technician was troubleshooting a desktop computer that would randomly crash. After running numerous diagnostic tests, he was unable to identify the cause of the problem.

On a whim, he decided to perform a visual inspection of the motherboard. He immediately noticed that several of the electrolytic capacitors near the CPU were swollen. He replaced the capacitors, and the computer stopped crashing.

This case illustrates the power of visual inspection. The technician could have spent hours running diagnostic tests, but the swollen capacitors provided a quick and easy solution.

Visual inspection is an essential troubleshooting technique that can often reveal obvious problems that would otherwise be missed. By training your eyes to spot these visual cues, you can save time, reduce frustration, and become a more effective electronics repair technician.

(5.3) Multimeter Mastery: Voltage, Current, Resistance Testing

While visual inspection is a powerful first step, it can only reveal so much. To truly understand what's happening inside an electronic circuit, you need to measure the electrical parameters: voltage, current, and resistance. The multimeter is your window into the invisible world of electricity, allowing you to quantify these fundamental properties and pinpoint the source of many electronic problems. Think of this section as your training manual for becoming fluent in the language of electricity, using the multimeter as your translator.

Safety First, Always: Respecting the Power

Before delving into the techniques of voltage, current, and resistance testing, it's critical to reinforce the importance of safety. Electricity can be dangerous, and it's essential to take precautions to protect yourself from electrical shock. Remember these rules:

- **Power Down the Circuit:** Whenever possible, disconnect the power from the circuit before making any measurements. This eliminates the risk of electrical shock.
- **Use Insulated Probes:** Use test probes with insulated handles to prevent accidental contact with live circuits.
- **Work in a Dry Environment:** Avoid working in wet or humid conditions, as water can conduct electricity.
- **Double-Check Your Settings:** Before connecting the probes to the circuit, double-check that the multimeter is set to the correct function and range.
- **Know Your Limits:** If you're not comfortable working with live circuits, seek guidance from a qualified technician.

Voltage Testing: Measuring the Electrical Potential

Voltage is the electrical potential difference between two points in a circuit, often described as the "electrical pressure" that drives current flow. Measuring voltage allows you to check whether a circuit is receiving the correct amount of power and to identify voltage drops that may indicate a faulty component or connection.

To measure voltage, set the multimeter to the voltage (V) setting. Most multimeters have separate settings for DC voltage (VDC) and AC voltage (VAC). Make sure to select the correct setting for the type of voltage you are measuring.

Connect the red probe (positive) to the point you want to measure, and the black probe (negative) to a reference point, typically the ground. The multimeter will display the voltage difference between the two points.

When measuring voltage, the multimeter is connected in *parallel* with the circuit. This means that the probes are connected across the component or circuit you are measuring, without interrupting the flow of current.

Current Testing: Measuring the Flow of Charge

Current is the flow of electrical charge through a circuit, measured in amperes (amps). Measuring current allows you to check whether a circuit is drawing the correct amount of power and to identify short circuits or other problems that may be causing excessive current draw.

To measure current, set the multimeter to the current (A) setting. Most multimeters have separate settings for DC current (ADC) and AC current (AAC). Make sure to select the correct setting for the type of current you are measuring. Also, be aware that most multimeters have a maximum current rating, typically 10 amps. Exceeding this rating can damage the multimeter.

Important Note: Measuring current is different than measuring voltage or resistance.

To measure current, you must *break* the circuit and insert the multimeter *in series* with the current flow. This means that you must disconnect one of the wires or components in the circuit and connect the multimeter probes to the two open ends. The current will then flow through the multimeter, allowing it to measure the current value.

Resistance Testing: Measuring Opposition to Current Flow

Resistance is the opposition to the flow of electrical current, measured in ohms (Ω). Measuring resistance allows you to check the value of resistors, test the continuity of wires and connections, and identify short circuits or open circuits.

To measure resistance, set the multimeter to the resistance (Ω) setting. Make sure the circuit is powered *off* before measuring resistance, as applying voltage to a resistor while measuring its resistance can damage the multimeter.

Connect the probes to the two ends of the component or circuit you want to measure. The multimeter will display the resistance value.

When measuring resistance, make sure that the component is isolated from the rest of the circuit. Other components in the circuit can affect the resistance reading.

Case Study: The Power Supply Puzzle – Voltage, Current, and Resistance to the Rescue

A technician was troubleshooting a malfunctioning power supply. The power supply was producing the correct output voltage, but it was overheating and shutting down after a few minutes.

The technician used a multimeter to measure the voltage, current, and resistance in the power supply circuit. He found that the output voltage was within the specified range, but the output current was much higher than it should have been.

He then used the multimeter to measure the resistance between various points in the circuit and found a short circuit in one of the capacitors. He replaced the capacitor, and the power supply stopped overheating.

This case illustrates the power of multimeter measurements. By systematically measuring voltage, current, and resistance, the technician was able to quickly identify the cause of the problem.

Practical Implementations - Making the Measurements Meaningful

Beyond simply knowing how to measure voltage, current, and resistance, it's important to understand how to interpret these measurements and use them to diagnose problems. Here are some practical tips:

- **Compare to Expected Values:** Always compare your measurements to the expected values, as indicated on the schematic or in the datasheet for the components.
- **Look for Voltage Drops:** A significant voltage drop across a component or connection can indicate a problem.
- **Check for Continuity:** Use the multimeter's continuity setting to check for broken wires or open circuits.
- **Identify Short Circuits:** Use the multimeter's resistance setting to check for short circuits. A very low resistance between two points that should not be connected indicates a short circuit.

Multimeter mastery is an essential skill for any electronics repair technician. By understanding how to use the multimeter to measure voltage, current, and resistance, you can diagnose a wide range of electronic problems and repair devices with confidence.

(5.4) Signal Tracing: Following the Flow

Imagine a river system. The water starts at a source and flows through tributaries, channels, and dams, ultimately reaching its destination. In electronics, signals are like that water, flowing through circuits, interacting with components, and performing specific functions. Signal tracing is the art of following these "rivers" of electrical information, tracking their characteristics to pinpoint where a signal is being lost, distorted, or otherwise corrupted. This technique is an extremely valuable skill that takes you beyond static measurements and into dynamic analysis. It does, however, require specific equipment.

Beyond Static Measurements: Understanding Dynamic Behavior

While measuring voltage, current, and resistance provides valuable information about the *state* of a circuit, it doesn't tell you anything about how signals are *behaving*. Signals are constantly changing, and their dynamic behavior is often critical to the proper functioning of the circuit. Signal tracing allows you to observe these dynamic characteristics and identify problems that would be impossible to detect with static measurements alone.

For example, a voltage signal might have the correct average voltage, but it could be distorted by noise, interference, or a faulty component. Signal tracing allows you to visualize these distortions and pinpoint their source.

The Tools of the Trade: Oscilloscopes and Logic Probes

Signal tracing requires specialized tools that can display and analyze dynamic signals. The two most common tools are oscilloscopes and logic probes.

- **Oscilloscope:** An oscilloscope is an electronic test instrument that displays a graph of voltage versus time. It allows you to visualize the shape, frequency, amplitude, and other characteristics of electrical signals. Oscilloscopes are indispensable for troubleshooting analog circuits, where the shape of the signal is often critical.

  An oscilloscope allows you to "see" the electricity flow through a circuit.

- **Logic Probe:** A logic probe is a simpler and less expensive tool that indicates the logic state (high or low) of a digital signal. Logic probes are useful for troubleshooting digital circuits, where the precise voltage level is less important than whether the signal is high or low.

  Logic probes are digital "yes" or "no" testers.

The choice between an oscilloscope and a logic probe depends on the type of circuit you are troubleshooting and the level of detail you need. For analog circuits, an oscilloscope is essential. For simple digital circuits, a logic probe may be sufficient.

The Signal Tracing Methodology: A Step-by-Step Approach

Signal tracing involves following a signal path through a circuit, monitoring the signal at various points, and comparing the measured signal characteristics to the expected characteristics. Here's a step-by-step approach:

1. **Identify the Signal Path:** Start by identifying the signal path you want to trace. This may involve consulting a schematic diagram or simply following the traces on the circuit board.
2. **Select a Starting Point:** Choose a starting point for your signal tracing. This is typically the input of the circuit or a point where the signal is known to be good.
3. **Connect the Probe:** Connect the oscilloscope or logic probe to the starting point.
4. **Observe the Signal:** Observe the signal characteristics. What is the shape, frequency, amplitude, and duty cycle of the signal? Does it match the expected characteristics?
5. **Move to the Next Point:** Move to the next point along the signal path and repeat steps 4 and 5.
6. **Compare the Signals:** Compare the signals at different points along the signal path. Are they the same? If not, what has changed?
7. **Isolate the Fault:** If the signal is being lost or distorted, isolate the section of the circuit that is causing the problem. This may involve testing individual components or replacing entire circuit blocks.

Interpreting the Signals: Unveiling the Clues

The key to successful signal tracing is knowing how to interpret the signals you are observing. Here are some common signal characteristics and what they can tell you:

- **Amplitude:** The amplitude of a signal is its strength or intensity. A low amplitude can indicate a weak signal source, a high impedance load, or a problem with the amplification circuitry.
- **Frequency:** The frequency of a signal is the number of cycles per second. An incorrect frequency can indicate a problem with the oscillator or timing circuitry.
- **Shape:** The shape of a signal can reveal a lot about its quality. A distorted signal can indicate a problem with the amplification circuitry, a faulty component, or interference from other signals.
- **Noise:** Noise is unwanted electrical interference that can corrupt signals. Excessive noise can indicate a problem with the power supply, grounding, or shielding.

Case Study: The Silent Amplifier - Following the Audio Signal

A technician was troubleshooting a silent audio amplifier. The amplifier had power, but there was no output signal.

The technician used an oscilloscope to trace the audio signal through the amplifier circuit. He started at the input and followed the signal through each stage of amplification.

He found that the signal was present at the input of the first amplifier stage, but it was completely absent at the output. This indicated that the first amplifier stage was faulty.

He then tested the components in the first amplifier stage and found that one of the transistors had failed. He replaced the transistor, and the amplifier started working perfectly again.

This case illustrates the power of signal tracing. By systematically following the audio signal through the circuit, the technician was able to quickly identify the faulty amplifier stage and repair the problem.

Signal tracing is a powerful technique that allows you to diagnose complex electronic problems by observing the dynamic behavior of signals. With practice and the right tools, you can become a master of signal tracing and unlock a new level of capabilities in electronics repair and troubleshooting.

(5.5) Using Schematics (Simplified): Understanding Circuit Diagrams

Think of a schematic diagram as a roadmap for an electronic circuit. Just as a roadmap shows you the paths between cities, a schematic shows you the connections between the components in a circuit. While a physical circuit board can be a confusing jumble of wires and components, a schematic provides a clear and organized representation of the circuit's structure.

While diving into complete schematic reading and design is beyond the scope of this book, it's important to note that even a basic understanding is an enormous aid to repair and troubleshooting. In this section, we'll cover the essential concepts to get you started, allowing you to follow signal paths, identify components, and understand the basic operation of a circuit. This is about equipping yourself with a crucial skill that unlocks a deeper level of understanding and repair capabilities.

Why Schematics Matter: A Clear View of the Circuit

Schematics are invaluable for several reasons:

- **Troubleshooting:** Schematics allow you to trace signal paths and identify potential points of failure. By comparing the actual circuit behavior to the schematic, you can quickly narrow down the source of a problem.
- **Understanding Circuit Operation:** Schematics provide a clear overview of how the different components in a circuit interact with each other. This understanding is essential for modifying or designing circuits.
- **Component Identification:** Schematics show the location and type of each component in the circuit, making it easier to identify and replace faulty components.
- **Reverse Engineering:** Schematics can be used to reverse engineer existing circuits, allowing you to understand how they work and to make modifications or improvements.

Basic Schematic Symbols: Learning the Language

Schematics use standardized symbols to represent different electronic components. Learning these symbols is like learning a new language. Here are some of the most common symbols you'll encounter:

- **Resistor:** Represented by a zigzag line or a rectangle.
- **Capacitor:** Represented by two parallel lines.
- **Inductor:** Represented by a coil of wire.
- **Diode:** Represented by a triangle pointing to a line.
- **Transistor:** Represented by a circle with three leads extending from it.
- **Integrated Circuit (IC):** Represented by a rectangle with multiple pins.
- **Ground:** Represented by a series of horizontal lines.
- **Voltage Source:** Represented by a circle with a plus sign and a minus sign.

Online resources provide comprehensive lists and explanations of schematic symbols.

Reading the Connections: Following the Lines

In a schematic, lines represent wires or traces that connect the components together. The lines show the path that electrical current takes through the circuit.

Connections between lines are typically indicated by a dot. If two lines cross without a dot, it means they are not connected. Understanding how lines connect components is crucial for following signal paths and understanding how the circuit works.

Understanding Basic Circuit Configurations

Schematics also show how components are arranged in the circuit. Certain common arrangements appear frequently.

- **Series Circuits** Components are connected end-to-end, so the same current flows through each.
- **Parallel Circuits** Components are connected side-by-side, so the voltage is the same across each, but the current divides between them.

Voltage and Ground: The Reference Points

Voltage and ground are the two reference points in a circuit. Voltage represents the electrical potential, while ground represents the zero-voltage reference point.

In schematics, voltage is typically indicated by a "+V" or "VCC" symbol, while ground is indicated by a ground symbol. Understanding the location of voltage and ground is essential for understanding how the circuit is powered.

Case Study: Using a Schematic to Repair a Radio

A radio enthusiast was repairing a vintage tube radio. The radio was producing a loud hum, but there was no audio signal.

The enthusiast obtained a schematic for the radio and used it to trace the audio signal through the circuit. He found that the signal was being lost in one of the amplifier stages.

He then used the schematic to identify the components in the faulty amplifier stage. He tested the components with a multimeter and found that one of the capacitors had failed. He replaced the capacitor, and the radio started working perfectly again.

From Mystery to Understanding

While becoming a schematic expert takes time and effort, even a basic understanding of schematics can greatly enhance your ability to troubleshoot and repair electronic devices. It empowers you to understand the circuit's operation, follow signal paths, identify components, and diagnose problems more effectively. With a schematic in hand, you can transform from a bewildered observer to a confident and capable repair technician.

Chapter 6: Smartphone & Tablet Repair

Welcome to Chapter 6, where we'll tackle the world of smartphone and tablet repair! These devices have become indispensable tools in our daily lives, so when they break down, it can be incredibly frustrating. But fear not! With the right knowledge, tools, and techniques, many common smartphone and tablet issues can be resolved at home, saving you time, money, and the hassle of sending your device off for professional repair.

Important Note: Smartphone and tablet repair can be delicate, and there is always a risk of damaging your device if you're not careful. Proceed with caution and follow the instructions carefully. Before beginning, back up your data. This chapter is designed to guide you through basic repairs, but some issues may require specialized tools and expertise.

(6.1) Common Smartphone Issues: Screen, Battery, Charging

Smartphones have become extensions of ourselves, our constant companions for communication, information, and entertainment. So, it's no surprise that when these devices malfunction, it can disrupt our daily lives significantly. While smartphones are marvels of engineering, they are also prone to certain common issues that can impact their functionality. Understanding these failure points – specifically screen damage, battery degradation, and charging problems – is crucial for effective troubleshooting and repair. Knowing the "enemy" is half the battle!

The Shattered Reality: Screen Damage and its Manifestations

A cracked or broken screen is, without a doubt, the most prevalent smartphone ailment. These incidents can range from hairline fractures to complete shattering, rendering the display unusable. The causes are often accidental: drops, impacts with hard surfaces, or excessive pressure in pockets or bags.

However, the consequences extend beyond mere cosmetic damage. A cracked screen can:

- **Impair Touch Functionality:** Cracks can disrupt the touch sensors, making it difficult or impossible to use certain parts of the screen.
- **Cause Display Issues:** Cracks can damage the underlying LCD or OLED panel, leading to dead pixels, discoloration, or flickering.
- **Expose Internal Components:** A severely shattered screen can expose the internal components of the phone to dust, moisture, and other contaminants, potentially causing further damage.
- **Create Safety Hazards:** Small shards of glass can detach from the screen, posing a risk of cuts and scrapes.

In recent years, manufacturers have been using more durable glass, such as Gorilla Glass, to improve screen resistance. However, even the toughest glass is not immune to damage.

Battery Blues: The Gradual Decline of Power

Battery degradation is another inevitable issue that affects all smartphones. Lithium-ion batteries, the type used in most smartphones, gradually lose their capacity over time and with each charge cycle. This means that the battery holds less charge, drains faster, and may eventually become unable to power on the device.

Several factors contribute to battery degradation:

- **Charge Cycles:** Each time a battery is fully charged and discharged, it loses a small amount of capacity.
- **Extreme Temperatures:** Exposing the battery to extreme heat or cold can accelerate degradation.
- **Overcharging:** Leaving the phone plugged in after it's fully charged can also damage the battery.
- **Fast Charging:** While convenient, fast charging can generate more heat and potentially degrade the battery faster over time.

The symptoms of battery degradation include:

- **Reduced Battery Life:** The phone needs to be charged more frequently.

- **Slow Charging:** The battery takes longer to charge.
- **Sudden Shutdowns:** The phone suddenly powers off, even when the battery indicator shows a significant charge remaining.
- **Swollen Battery:** In rare cases, a severely degraded battery can swell, posing a fire hazard.

The Unreliable Connection: Charging Problems and Their Sources

Charging problems are another common source of frustration for smartphone users. These issues can manifest in various ways, such as the phone not charging at all, charging very slowly, or intermittently disconnecting from the charger.

The causes of charging problems can be varied:

- **Faulty Charging Cable:** The charging cable is often the weakest link in the charging chain. Cables can become frayed, damaged, or simply worn out over time.
- **Damaged Charging Port:** The charging port on the phone can become clogged with lint, dust, or debris. The pins inside the port can also become bent or damaged.
- **Faulty Charging Adapter:** The charging adapter may not be providing enough power to charge the phone.
- **Software Issues:** In some cases, charging problems can be caused by software glitches.
- **Battery Problems:** A severely degraded battery may not be able to accept a charge.
- **Motherboard Damage:** The charging circuitry on the motherboard can become damaged by power surges or physical impact.

Case Study: A Quick Fix for a Slow Charging Phone

A smartphone user was complaining that their phone was charging extremely slowly. They had tried different charging cables and adapters, but the problem persisted. Before taking the phone in for repair, they decided to try cleaning the charging port with a small brush.

To their surprise, they removed a significant amount of lint and debris from the port. After cleaning the port, the phone started charging at its normal speed. This simple fix saved them a trip to the repair shop and the cost of a new charging port.

Understanding these common smartphone issues – screen damage, battery degradation, and charging problems – is the first step towards becoming a proficient smartphone repair technician. By recognizing the symptoms, understanding the causes, and implementing appropriate solutions, you can extend the life of your device and save yourself time, money, and frustration.

(6.2) Disassembly & Reassembly: Best Practices

Disassembling a smartphone or tablet can feel like performing surgery on a miniature electronic patient. Just like in surgery, precision, care, and a clear understanding of the anatomy are crucial for success. Disassembly and reassembly are the gateway to most smartphone and tablet repairs, making it essential to develop a set of best practices that minimize the risk of damage and ensure a smooth repair process. This isn't about brute force; it's about delicate manipulation and methodical organization.

The Foundation: Preparation and the Right Tools

Before you even think about opening the device, proper preparation is essential. This includes gathering the right tools, creating a clean and organized workspace, and understanding the device's construction.

The right tools can make the difference between a successful repair and a disastrous one. Here are some essential tools to have on hand:

- **Specialized Screwdrivers:** Smartphones and tablets use a variety of small, specialized screws, including Phillips, Torx, Pentalobe, and Tri-Point. A high-quality precision screwdriver set with multiple bits is essential. Magnetic tips are extremely useful for holding onto the tiny screws.
- **Plastic Opening Tools:** Plastic opening tools, such as spudgers, picks, and opening levers, are used to pry open cases and disconnect connectors without scratching or damaging the plastic. Avoid using metal tools, as they can easily damage the device.
- **Heat Gun or Hairdryer:** Many smartphones and tablets use adhesive to secure the screen or back cover. A heat gun or hairdryer can be used to soften the adhesive before attempting to pry open the device.

- **Suction Cup:** A suction cup can be used to lift the screen or back cover after the adhesive has been softened.
- **Tweezers:** Fine-tipped tweezers are essential for handling small components and connectors.
- **Magnetic Project Mat or Organizer:** A magnetic project mat or a small parts organizer is crucial for keeping track of the tiny screws and other small parts that you remove during disassembly. This will prevent them from getting lost or mixed up.

Creating a clean and organized workspace is also important. Choose a well-lit area with a stable surface. Clear away any clutter and make sure you have plenty of room to work.

The Disassembly Process: A Step-by-Step Approach

With the right tools and a well-prepared workspace, you're ready to begin the disassembly process. Here are some best practices to follow:

1. **Consult a Repair Guide:** Never attempt to disassemble a smartphone or tablet without consulting a reputable repair guide. Websites like iFixit offer detailed, step-by-step instructions and photos for a wide variety of devices. Following a repair guide will help you avoid making mistakes and damaging the device.
2. **Power Off the Device:** Always power off the device before disassembling it. This will prevent accidental short circuits and damage to the components.
3. **Apply Heat (If Necessary):** If the device uses adhesive to secure the screen or back cover, apply heat to soften the adhesive. Use a heat gun or hairdryer on a low setting and move it around the edges of the device for several minutes.
4. **Use Plastic Opening Tools:** Insert a plastic opening tool into the seam between the case halves and gently pry them apart. Work your way around the edges of the device, applying gentle pressure to release the adhesive.
5. **Be Careful with Cables:** Pay close attention to any cables that connect the screen, battery, or other components to the motherboard. Use a plastic spudger to gently pry the connectors loose. Avoid pulling on the wires, as this can damage the connectors.
6. **Organize Your Screws:** As you remove screws, place them in a magnetic project mat or small parts organizer, keeping track of

where each screw came from. This will make reassembly much easier.

The Reassembly Process: Putting It All Back Together

Reassembly is just as important as disassembly. Follow these best practices to ensure that the device is properly reassembled:

1. **Follow the Repair Guide:** Follow the reassembly instructions in the repair guide carefully.
2. **Connect All Cables:** Make sure that all cables are properly connected before closing the device.
3. **Tighten Screws Carefully:** Tighten the screws carefully, avoiding over-tightening. Over-tightening can strip the screw threads or damage the components.
4. **Test Before Closing:** Before fully closing the device, test the repaired component to make sure it is working properly.
5. **Apply New Adhesive (If Necessary):** If you removed the screen or back cover, apply new adhesive to secure it in place.
6. **Clean the Device:** Clean the device to remove any fingerprints or smudges.

Case Study: The Forgotten Screw - A Costly Mistake

A smartphone user was replacing the battery in their phone. They carefully followed a repair guide, but they forgot to replace one of the screws that secured the battery connector to the motherboard.

After reassembling the phone, they turned it on and immediately smelled burning plastic. The missing screw had allowed the battery connector to come loose, causing a short circuit that damaged the motherboard. The phone was beyond repair.

This case illustrates the importance of following the repair guide carefully and making sure that all screws and components are properly installed.

Disassembly and reassembly are essential skills for any smartphone or tablet repair technician. By following these best practices, you can minimize the risk of damage and ensure a smooth and successful repair process.

(6.3) Screen Replacement: A Detailed Guide

A cracked or shattered screen is arguably the most common and visually jarring issue that plagues smartphones and tablets. While seemingly catastrophic, a screen replacement is a repair that, with patience and the right guidance, can be successfully performed at home. This section will provide a detailed, step-by-step guide to screen replacement, emphasizing the crucial techniques and precautions necessary for a successful outcome.

Before You Begin: Preparation and Essential Tools

Before you even think about touching your device, proper preparation is paramount. This includes gathering the necessary tools, finding a reliable repair guide, and creating a clean and organized workspace.

- **The Right Tools:** As mentioned previously, you'll need a specialized screwdriver set, plastic opening tools (spudgers, picks), a heat gun or hairdryer, a suction cup, and tweezers. A screen removal plier is useful as well.
- **A Reliable Repair Guide:** Websites like iFixit offer detailed, step-by-step instructions and photos for a wide variety of devices. Find a guide specifically for your device model and follow it carefully.
- **A Clean and Organized Workspace:** Choose a well-lit area with a stable surface. Clear away any clutter and use a magnetic project mat or small parts organizer to keep track of the screws and other small parts.
- **A Static-Free Environment:** Work in an environment free from static electricity to avoid damaging sensitive components.

Step 1: Power Down and Protect Yourself

Always begin by powering off the device to prevent any electrical mishaps. Remove your sim card and SD card to prevent damage to them. Before you begin the screen replacement, ground yourself with an anti-static wrist strap to protect the internal components from electrostatic discharge (ESD).

Step 2: Applying Heat to Soften the Adhesive

Many smartphones and tablets use adhesive to secure the screen to the frame. Applying heat to the edges of the screen will soften the adhesive and make it easier to pry open the device.

Use a heat gun or hairdryer on a low setting and move it around the edges of the screen for several minutes. Be careful not to overheat the screen, as this can damage the LCD or OLED panel. A temperature of around 80-100°C (176-212°F) is generally sufficient.

Step 3: Creating an Opening with a Suction Cup

After applying heat, use a suction cup to create a small opening between the screen and the frame. Position the suction cup near the bottom edge of the screen and apply firm pressure.

Gently lift the suction cup to create a small gap. Be careful not to lift the screen too far, as this can damage the flex cables that connect the screen to the motherboard.

Step 4: Prying Open the Device with Plastic Tools

Insert a plastic opening tool (spudger or pick) into the gap created by the suction cup. Gently slide the plastic opening tool around the edges of the screen, separating the adhesive.

Be patient and apply gentle pressure. If you encounter resistance, apply more heat to soften the adhesive.

Step 5: Disconnecting the Flex Cables

Once the screen is separated from the frame, carefully lift it up, being mindful of the flex cables that connect it to the motherboard. Use a plastic spudger to gently pry the connectors loose from their sockets.

Be extremely careful not to damage the connectors or the cables. If a cable is stuck, try using a heat gun or hairdryer to soften the adhesive underneath it.

Step 6: Removing the Old Screen and Cleaning the Frame

After disconnecting the flex cables, carefully remove the old screen from the frame. Use a plastic scraper or a cotton swab dipped in isopropyl alcohol to remove any remaining adhesive from the frame.

Make sure the frame is clean and free of any debris before installing the new screen.

Step 7: Installing the New Screen

Carefully align the new screen with the frame and press it into place. Connect the flex cables to the motherboard, making sure they are securely seated.

Step 8: Testing Before Final Assembly

Before fully reassembling the device, power it on and test the new screen to make sure it is working properly. Check the touch sensitivity, brightness, and color accuracy.

If everything is working correctly, you can proceed to the final assembly.

Step 9: Reassembling the Device and Applying New Adhesive

Follow the reassembly instructions in the repair guide carefully. Apply new adhesive to the frame before attaching the screen to the frame to secure a reliable connection. Carefully tighten the screws and press the screen in firmly.

Step 10: Final Testing and Cleaning

Power on the device and test all functions to make sure everything is working correctly. Clean the screen with a microfiber cloth to remove any fingerprints or smudges.

Case Study: A Cautionary Tale of a Rushed Repair

An eager DIYer attempted to replace a cracked iPhone screen without consulting a repair guide. In his haste, he used a metal screwdriver to pry open the phone, scratching the frame and damaging a flex cable. He then used excessive force to connect the new screen, bending several pins on the connector.

As a result, the phone was completely unusable, and he had to take it to a professional repair shop to fix his mistakes. This case illustrates the importance of proper preparation, following a repair guide, and using the right tools.

Replacing a smartphone or tablet screen requires patience, precision, and attention to detail. By following these steps and taking the necessary precautions, you can successfully replace your screen and restore your device to its former glory.

(6.4) Battery Replacement: Choosing the Right Battery

As we discussed earlier, battery degradation is a common and unavoidable issue in smartphones and tablets. Replacing a worn-out battery can breathe new life into your device, restoring its original battery life and performance. However, selecting the right replacement battery is crucial for ensuring safety, compatibility, and long-term reliability. This section will provide a comprehensive guide to choosing the right battery, helping you navigate the often-confusing world of replacement batteries and make an informed decision. The choices are extensive and not always equivalent.

Beyond the Specs: Understanding Battery Compatibility

The most important factor in choosing a replacement battery is compatibility. Using an incompatible battery can damage your device, cause it to malfunction, or even create a safety hazard.

To ensure compatibility, start by identifying the exact model number of your smartphone or tablet. This information can typically be found on the device itself, in the settings menu, or on the original packaging.

Once you know the model number, look for replacement batteries that are specifically designed for that model. Many online retailers and battery manufacturers offer compatibility charts or search tools to help you find the right battery.

Pay close attention to the battery specifications, including:

- **Voltage:** The voltage of the replacement battery must match the voltage of the original battery.
- **Capacity:** The capacity of the battery is measured in milliampere-hours (mAh). A higher capacity battery will typically provide

longer battery life. However, it's important to choose a battery with a capacity that is within the recommended range for your device.

- **Dimensions:** The dimensions of the replacement battery must match the dimensions of the original battery. If the battery is too large or too small, it may not fit properly in the device.
- **Connector Type:** The connector type of the replacement battery must match the connector type on the motherboard.

The Pitfalls of Cheap Batteries: Quality and Safety Concerns

While it may be tempting to save money by purchasing a cheap replacement battery, this is often a risky proposition. Low-quality batteries may not meet the stated specifications, may be prone to premature failure, and may even pose a safety hazard.

Cheap batteries may contain substandard components, lack proper safety circuitry, or be manufactured using unethical labor practices. They may also be more likely to overheat, swell, or even explode.

It's always best to purchase replacement batteries from reputable brands or authorized distributors. These batteries may cost more, but they are more likely to be of high quality and to meet safety standards. Look for batteries with certifications.

Decoding Battery Certifications

One way to assess the quality and safety of a replacement battery is to look for certifications from reputable organizations. Some common certifications include:

- **UL Certification:** Indicates that the battery has been tested and meets Underwriters Laboratories safety standards.
- **CE Marking:** Indicates that the battery meets European safety, health, and environmental protection requirements.
- **RoHS Compliance:** Indicates that the battery complies with the Restriction of Hazardous Substances directive, which restricts the use of certain hazardous materials in electronic products.

Ethical Considerations: Supporting Responsible Manufacturing

When choosing a replacement battery, it's also important to consider the ethical implications of your purchase. Many electronic components are manufactured in factories with poor working conditions and low wages. By purchasing batteries from reputable brands that prioritize ethical sourcing, you can help support responsible manufacturing practices.

Look for brands that are transparent about their supply chain and that have certifications from organizations that promote fair labor practices.

Case Study: The Dangers of a Counterfeit Battery

A smartphone user purchased a replacement battery online for a very low price. The battery was labeled as being manufactured by a reputable brand, but it turned out to be a counterfeit.

A few weeks after installing the battery, the phone started to overheat. The user ignored the warnings, and one day the battery exploded, causing a fire that damaged their home. This case illustrates the dangers of purchasing counterfeit or low-quality batteries.

Choosing the right replacement battery for your smartphone or tablet is a crucial decision that can impact the safety, performance, and longevity of your device. By following these guidelines and taking the necessary precautions, you can make an informed decision and ensure a safe and successful battery replacement.

(6.5) Troubleshooting Charging Problems

A smartphone or tablet that won't charge is more than an inconvenience; it's a lifeline severed. The ability to power up and stay connected is fundamental to the functionality of these devices, making charging issues a particularly frustrating problem. But don't despair! Many charging problems can be diagnosed and resolved with a methodical approach and a basic understanding of the potential causes. This section will provide you with a step-by-step guide to troubleshooting charging problems, empowering you to identify the root cause and restore your device to its full charging potential. It's like being a detective searching for a power leak.

The Importance of a Systematic Approach: Ruling Out the Simple Stuff First

Before diving into complex repairs, it's essential to start with the simplest and most common causes of charging problems. This will save you time and prevent you from unnecessarily disassembling your device. Start with the basics.

Step 1: The Obvious Suspects - Cable, Adapter, and Wall Socket

The first step is to rule out the external components: the charging cable, the charging adapter, and the wall socket.

- **Try a Different Cable:** Charging cables are prone to damage and wear, especially at the connector ends. Try using a different charging cable that you know is working properly.
- **Try a Different Adapter:** The charging adapter may not be providing enough power to charge the phone. Try using a different adapter, preferably one that is specifically designed for your device. Check the adapter to make sure it is outputting the correct voltage.
- **Try a Different Wall Socket:** The wall socket may not be providing power. Try plugging the charger into a different wall socket.
- **Check the Cable for Damage:** Visually inspect the charging cable for any signs of damage, such as frayed wires, cracked insulation, or bent connectors. If you see any damage, replace the cable.
- **Test the Adapter with Another Device:** If possible, test the charging adapter with another device to see if it is working properly.

Step 2: The Port of Entry - Examining the Charging Port

If the cable, adapter, and wall socket are working properly, the next step is to examine the charging port on the device.

- **Clean the Charging Port:** The charging port can become clogged with lint, dust, or debris, preventing the charging cable from making a good connection. Use a small brush, a toothpick, or a can of compressed air to gently clean the charging port.
- **Check for Bent Pins:** The pins inside the charging port can become bent or damaged, preventing the charging cable from making a proper connection. Use a magnifying glass to inspect the pins for any damage. If you see any bent pins, try to gently straighten them with a small needle or pin.

- **Test Another Device:** If possible, connect the device to a computer and see if the computer recognizes it. This can help determine if the charging port is working at all.

Step 3: Software Suspects - Ruling Out Glitches

Software glitches can sometimes interfere with the charging process. Before assuming a hardware problem, try the following:

- **Restart the Device:** A simple restart can often resolve minor software glitches.
- **Update the Operating System:** Make sure that your device is running the latest version of the operating system. Software updates often include bug fixes that can resolve charging problems.
- **Check for App Interference:** Some apps can interfere with the charging process. Try uninstalling any recently installed apps to see if that resolves the problem.
- **Factory Reset:** In some extreme circumstances, a factory reset may help. However, be sure to back up your data first.

Step 4: Battery Assessment - Gauging Battery Health

A degraded or damaged battery can also cause charging problems. If your battery is old or has been subjected to extreme temperatures, it may be time to replace it.

- **Check Battery Health (if available):** Some smartphones and tablets have a built-in battery health indicator that provides information about the battery's capacity and condition. Check this indicator to see if the battery needs to be replaced.
- **Look for Swelling:** A swollen battery is a clear sign of damage and should be replaced immediately.
- **Consult a Repair Professional:** If you suspect that the battery is the problem, it's best to consult a repair professional for assistance. Replacing a battery can be dangerous if you're not careful.

Step 5: The Motherboard Maze - When Hardware Requires a Pro

If you've ruled out all the simpler causes, the problem may lie on the motherboard. This often requires specialized tools and expertise to diagnose and repair. This is where consulting a professional may be necessary.

- **Check the Fuses** Use a multimeter to check the fuse for continuity.
- **Look for Damaged Components:** Look for any burned or damaged components near the charging port or on the charging circuitry.
- **Consult a Schematic:** If you're comfortable reading schematics, you can use a schematic diagram to trace the charging circuit and identify potential points of failure.

Case Study: From No Charge to a Clean Port

A tablet user was experiencing intermittent charging problems. The tablet would sometimes charge, but other times it would not. They tried different cables and adapters, but the problem persisted.

After consulting a repair guide, they decided to examine the charging port. Using a magnifying glass, they noticed that there was a small piece of debris lodged inside the port. They carefully removed the debris with a small needle, and the tablet started charging reliably again.

This case illustrates the importance of examining the charging port for any signs of damage or debris. A simple cleaning can often resolve charging problems.

Troubleshooting charging problems requires a systematic approach, a keen eye for detail, and a basic understanding of electronics. By following these steps, you can identify the root cause of many charging issues and restore your smartphone or tablet to its full charging potential.

(6.6) Button & Speaker Repair

While touchscreens dominate the user interface of smartphones and tablets, physical buttons and speakers remain essential for certain functions. When these components malfunction, it can significantly impact the usability and enjoyment of your device. This section provides a practical guide to diagnosing and resolving common issues with buttons and speakers, empowering you to restore these important functions and extend the life of your device. It's about getting back the tactile feel and the audio experience you rely on.

The Tactile Connection: Troubleshooting Button Issues

Physical buttons, such as power buttons, volume buttons, and home buttons, are subjected to a lot of wear and tear. Over time, they can become unresponsive, stuck, or difficult to press.

The causes of button problems can be varied:

- **Dirt and Debris:** Dirt, dust, and lint can accumulate around the button, preventing it from making proper contact with the underlying switch.
- **Physical Damage:** The button itself can become cracked, broken, or dislodged.
- **Worn-Out Switch:** The switch beneath the button can wear out over time, becoming less responsive.
- **Liquid Damage:** Liquid spills can damage the button mechanism or corrode the electrical contacts.

Here's a systematic approach to troubleshooting button issues:

1. **External Cleaning:** Start by cleaning the button and the surrounding area with a soft brush or a cotton swab dipped in isopropyl alcohol. Gently scrub around the button to remove any dirt or debris.
2. **Compressed Air:** Use compressed air to blow out any debris that may be lodged inside the button mechanism.
3. **Check for Physical Damage:** Inspect the button for any signs of physical damage, such as cracks, breaks, or missing pieces.
4. **Test the Button with a Multimeter (Advanced):** If you're comfortable using a multimeter, you can test the button switch for continuity. Set the multimeter to the continuity setting and connect the probes to the button's terminals. Press the button; the multimeter should beep, indicating continuity. If there is no continuity, the switch is likely faulty.
5. **Check Flex Cable and Connectors:** If the button presses but the system doesn't respond, there may be a problem with the button's flex cable and connectors. Use a repair guide to disassemble the device and inspect these connections. Re-seat the flex cable connector or if there is obvious damage, replace the flex cable.
6. **Software Check:** Rarely, the issue can be software-related. Perform a soft reset on your device, and ensure that the operating system is up to date.

If the button is damaged or the switch is faulty, you may need to replace the entire button assembly. This typically involves disassembling the device and soldering a new button assembly to the motherboard. This is an advanced repair that requires specialized tools and skills.

The Sound of Silence: Diagnosing Speaker Problems

Speakers are essential for listening to music, watching videos, and making phone calls. When speakers malfunction, the audio output can become muffled, distorted, or completely silent.

The causes of speaker problems can include:

- **Dirt and Debris:** Dirt, dust, and lint can accumulate inside the speaker grill, blocking the sound.
- **Water Damage:** Water can damage the speaker cone or corrode the electrical connections.
- **Physical Damage:** The speaker cone can become torn or punctured, or the speaker wires can become disconnected.
- **Software Issues:** Audio settings can be accidentally configured to mute the speaker.

Here's a systematic approach to troubleshooting speaker issues:

1. **External Cleaning:** Start by cleaning the speaker grill with a soft brush or a cotton swab. Gently scrub the grill to remove any dirt or debris.
2. **Check Audio Settings:** Make sure that the volume is turned up and that the speaker is not muted. Check the audio settings in the device's settings menu.
3. **Test with Different Audio Sources:** Try playing audio from different apps or sources to see if the problem is specific to one app or source.
4. **Check for Headphone Mode:** Sometimes, the device may mistakenly think that headphones are plugged in, even when they are not. Plug in and unplug headphones a few times to try and reset the audio output.
5. **Look for Liquid Damage:** Inspect the device for any signs of liquid damage. If the device has been exposed to water, try drying it out completely.

6. **Test the Speaker with a Multimeter (Advanced):** Set the multimeter to the ohms (Ω) setting and connect the probes to the speaker terminals. A good speaker should show a resistance of a few ohms. If the multimeter displays "OL" (overload) or a very high resistance, the speaker is likely open and needs to be replaced.

If the speaker is damaged or not functioning, you may need to replace the entire speaker assembly. This typically involves disassembling the device and soldering a new speaker to the motherboard. This is an advanced repair that requires specialized tools and skills.

Case Study: A Simple Cleaning Saves a Speaker

A tablet user was complaining that the speaker on their tablet was muffled and distorted. They tried adjusting the volume settings, but the problem persisted.

Before taking the tablet in for repair, they decided to try cleaning the speaker grill with a small brush. To their surprise, they removed a significant amount of dust and lint from the grill. After cleaning the grill, the speaker sounded clear and crisp again.

This case illustrates the importance of starting with the simplest solutions. A simple cleaning can often resolve speaker problems.

Troubleshooting button and speaker issues requires a combination of careful observation, systematic testing, and a bit of luck. By following these steps, you can identify the root cause of many problems and restore the functionality of these important components.

Chapter 7: Laptop & Computer Repair

Welcome to Chapter 7, where we'll dive into the world of laptop and computer repair! These machines are essential for work, education, and entertainment, so when they start acting up, it can be incredibly disruptive. The good news is that many common laptop and computer issues can be diagnosed and resolved at home, saving you time, money, and the hassle of taking your machine to a repair shop.

Important Note: Laptop and computer repair can involve working with sensitive components, so it's important to proceed with caution and follow the instructions carefully. Before beginning any repair, back up your data. This chapter is designed to guide you through basic repairs, but some issues may require specialized tools and expertise.

(7.1) Common Laptop Issues: Overheating, Slow Performance, Display Problems

Laptops have become essential tools for productivity, communication, and entertainment. However, like any complex machine, they are prone to certain common issues that can significantly impact their performance and usability. Overheating, slow performance, and display problems are among the most frequent complaints from laptop users. Understanding these issues is the first step towards effective troubleshooting and repair. Think of this as becoming familiar with the "usual suspects" in the world of laptop malfunctions.

The Silent Killer: Overheating and its Ripple Effects

Overheating is a insidious problem that can have a wide range of negative effects on your laptop. It's often a gradual process, starting with subtle performance slowdowns and eventually leading to system crashes, data loss, and even permanent hardware damage.

The causes of overheating are often related to the laptop's cooling system:

- **Dust Accumulation:** Dust can accumulate in the heatsink and fan, blocking airflow and reducing the cooling efficiency.
- **Dried Thermal Paste:** The thermal paste that transfers heat from the CPU and GPU to the heatsink can dry out over time, reducing its effectiveness.
- **Blocked Vents:** Covering the laptop's vents can restrict airflow and cause the laptop to overheat.
- **Demanding Tasks:** Running demanding applications, such as games or video editing software, can generate a lot of heat.
- **Ambient Temperature:** Using the laptop in a hot environment can also contribute to overheating.

The symptoms of overheating can include:

- **Slow Performance:** The laptop may become sluggish and unresponsive.
- **Loud Fan Noise:** The fan may run constantly and at a high speed.
- **System Crashes:** The laptop may suddenly crash or freeze.
- **Unexpected Shutdowns:** The laptop may suddenly shut down without warning.
- **Physical Discomfort:** The laptop may become uncomfortably hot to the touch.

The Tortoise Effect: Decoding Slow Performance

Slow performance is a frustrating problem that can make even simple tasks feel like a chore. There are many potential causes of slow performance, ranging from software issues to hardware limitations.

- **Full Hard Drive:** A hard drive that is nearly full can slow down the system significantly.
- **Fragmented Hard Drive:** Over time, files on the hard drive can become fragmented, making it slower to access them.
- **Malware:** Malware can consume system resources and slow down the system.
- **Outdated Drivers:** Outdated drivers can cause compatibility issues and performance problems.
- **Too Many Startup Programs:** Programs that run automatically at startup can consume system resources and slow down the boot process.

- **Insufficient RAM:** If the laptop doesn't have enough RAM, it may struggle to run multiple programs at once.
- **Old or Slow Hard Drive:** Traditional mechanical hard drives are much slower than solid-state drives (SSDs).

The symptoms of slow performance can include:

- **Slow Boot Times:** The laptop takes a long time to start up.
- **Slow Application Loading:** Applications take a long time to load.
- **Unresponsive System:** The system becomes sluggish and unresponsive.
- **Frequent Freezing:** The system freezes frequently.

Seeing is Believing: Identifying Display Problems

Display problems can range from minor annoyances to complete showstoppers, making it impossible to use the laptop.

- **Blank Screen:** The screen is completely black, even when the laptop is turned on.
- **Flickering Screen:** The screen flickers or flashes intermittently.
- **Distorted Image:** The image on the screen is distorted, with lines, patterns, or unusual colors.
- **Dead Pixels:** Small black or colored dots appear on the screen.
- **Backlight Issues:** The screen is dim or difficult to see, even at maximum brightness.

The causes of display problems can include:

- **Loose or Damaged Cable:** The cable connecting the screen to the motherboard may be loose or damaged.
- **Graphics Driver Issues:** Outdated or corrupted graphics drivers can cause display problems.
- **Faulty Graphics Card:** The graphics card may be failing.
- **Damaged LCD or LED Panel:** The LCD or LED panel may be damaged due to impact or pressure.
- **Inverter Failure**: LCD screens use an inverter to supply power to the screen.

Case Study: The Overheating Laptop That Refused to Die

A student was using an old laptop for schoolwork. The laptop was constantly overheating, and the fan was running at full speed. The student was about to give up on the laptop and buy a new one when they decided to try cleaning the cooling system.

They carefully disassembled the laptop and used compressed air to clean the heatsink and fan. They were amazed at how much dust had accumulated inside. After cleaning the cooling system, the laptop stopped overheating and ran much faster. The student was able to continue using the laptop for another year, saving hundreds of dollars.

Understanding these common laptop issues – overheating, slow performance, and display problems – is the foundation for effective troubleshooting and repair. By recognizing the symptoms, understanding the causes, and implementing appropriate solutions, you can extend the life of your laptop and keep it running smoothly for years to come.

(7.2) Disassembly & Reassembly: Laptop-Specific Tips

While the general principles of disassembly and reassembly apply to both laptops and desktop computers, laptops present a unique set of challenges due to their compact size, intricate design, and delicate components. Navigating the labyrinthine interiors of a laptop requires a more nuanced approach than a desktop. This section will provide you with laptop-specific tips and best practices to ensure a smooth and successful repair process, minimizing the risk of damage and maximizing your chances of a positive outcome. It's about learning the subtle art of laptop anatomy.

The Laptop Landscape: Understanding the Key Differences

Compared to desktop computers, laptops are characterized by:

- **Miniaturization:** Components are smaller and more densely packed.
- **Integration:** Components are often integrated into the motherboard, making them more difficult to replace.
- **Fragility:** Components are more delicate and susceptible to damage.

- **Complexity:** The internal layout is more complex and varies significantly between models.
- **Proprietary Parts:** Laptops often use proprietary parts that are not interchangeable between different brands or models.

These characteristics demand a more cautious and methodical approach to disassembly and reassembly.

Before You Begin: Preparation is Paramount

As with any electronics repair, proper preparation is crucial. However, in the case of laptops, it's even more important due to the increased complexity and fragility of the components.

- **Find a Reliable Repair Guide:** Never attempt to disassemble a laptop without consulting a reputable repair guide. Websites like iFixit offer detailed, step-by-step instructions and photos for a wide variety of laptop models.
- **Gather the Right Tools:** Make sure you have all the necessary tools before you begin. This includes specialized screwdrivers, plastic opening tools, a heat gun or hairdryer, and a magnetic project mat.
- **Create a Detailed Diagram:** Before disassembling the laptop, create a detailed diagram showing the location of all the screws, cables, and connectors. This will make reassembly much easier. You can physically draw on a printed image or use a digital design tool on a tablet.
- **Take Pictures:** Take pictures of each step of the disassembly process. This will provide a visual reference to help you remember where everything goes.
- **Label Everything:** Label all the cables and connectors with tape and a marker. This will help you avoid confusion during reassembly.
- **Ground Yourself:** Use an anti-static wrist strap to prevent static electricity from damaging the components.

Disassembly Strategies: Navigating the Internal Maze

Disassembling a laptop requires a methodical approach and a keen eye for detail. Here are some laptop-specific tips:

- **Remove the Battery First:** Always remove the battery before disassembling a laptop. This will prevent accidental short circuits and damage to the components.
- **Start with the Easy Stuff:** Start by removing the easy-to-access components, such as the hard drive, RAM, and optical drive. This will make it easier to access the more difficult components.
- **Be Careful with the Keyboard:** Laptop keyboards are often attached to the case with delicate clips. Use a plastic opening tool to gently pry the keyboard loose, being careful not to break the clips.
- **Watch Out for Hidden Screws:** Laptops often have hidden screws under rubber feet, stickers, or other components. Make sure to remove all screws before attempting to separate the case halves.
- **Be Gentle with the Screen:** Laptop screens are very fragile. Handle them with care and avoid applying excessive pressure.
- **Document Cable Routing:** Make a note of how cables are routed. They may be deliberately routed in a certain way to ensure they don't come into contact with other components.

Reassembly Tactics: Putting the Puzzle Back Together

Reassembling a laptop can be just as challenging as disassembling it. Here are some tips to make the process easier:

- **Follow Your Diagram and Photos:** Use the diagram and photos you created during disassembly to guide you through the reassembly process.
- **Connect All Cables Carefully:** Make sure that all cables are properly connected before closing the case.
- **Tighten Screws Gently:** Tighten the screws gently, avoiding over-tightening. Over-tightening can strip the screw threads or damage the components.
- **Test Before Closing Completely:** Before fully closing the case, test the laptop to make sure that everything is working properly.
- **Clean Before Reassembling:** Ensure that the heat sink and fan are clean before reassembling.

Case Study: The Overheated Laptop Saved by Careful Disassembly

A laptop user was experiencing frequent overheating problems. They suspected that the cooling system was clogged with dust, but they were hesitant to disassemble the laptop for fear of damaging it.

After consulting a repair guide and watching several YouTube videos, they decided to attempt the repair. They carefully followed the instructions, taking pictures of each step of the disassembly process.

They found that the heatsink was completely clogged with dust. They cleaned the heatsink with compressed air and reassembled the laptop. The overheating problems were resolved, and the laptop ran much cooler.

This case illustrates the importance of preparation, following a repair guide, and documenting the disassembly process.

Disassembling and reassembling laptops requires patience, precision, and a methodical approach. By following these laptop-specific tips and best practices, you can minimize the risk of damage and increase your chances of a successful repair.

(7.3) RAM & Storage Upgrades: Boosting Performance

Is your laptop or computer feeling sluggish? Are applications taking forever to load? Are you constantly running out of storage space? If so, upgrading the RAM or storage can provide a significant boost in performance, making your machine feel like new again. These are relatively straightforward upgrades that can yield noticeable results, breathing new life into an aging system or maximizing the potential of a newer one. Think of this section as your guide to unleashing the hidden potential of your machine.

The Memory Boost: Unleashing Multitasking Power

Random Access Memory (RAM) is the short-term memory that your computer uses to store data and instructions that it is actively using. The more RAM you have, the more programs you can run simultaneously without experiencing performance slowdowns. Insufficient RAM is one of the most common causes of slow performance.

Upgrading the RAM can improve the speed and responsiveness of your system, especially when running multiple programs at once, working with large files, or playing demanding games.

Before upgrading the RAM, you need to determine the following:

- **RAM Type:** Determine the type of RAM that your laptop or computer uses. Common types include DDR3, DDR4, and DDR5. This information can typically be found in the system specifications or by using a tool like CPU-Z.
- **Maximum Capacity:** Determine the maximum amount of RAM that your laptop or computer can support. This information can also be found in the system specifications or by consulting the motherboard manufacturer's website.
- **Number of Slots:** Determine the number of RAM slots available in your laptop or computer. Some laptops have only one RAM slot, while others have two or more.
- **Speed:** Look for a RAM with the correct speed rating for your system.

To install the new RAM, follow these steps:

1. **Power Off and Disconnect:** Power off your computer and unplug it from the power outlet.
2. **Ground Yourself:** Use an anti-static wrist strap to prevent static electricity from damaging the components.
3. **Open the Case:** Open the computer case or the RAM compartment on your laptop.
4. **Locate the RAM Slots:** Locate the RAM slots on the motherboard.
5. **Insert the RAM Modules:** Align the notch on the RAM module with the notch on the RAM slot and press down firmly until the clips on either side of the slot click into place.
6. **Close the Case:** Close the computer case or the RAM compartment on your laptop.

The Storage Revolution: SSDs and the Speed of Light

Solid-state drives (SSDs) have revolutionized storage technology, offering significantly faster performance than traditional mechanical hard drives. Replacing a traditional hard drive with an SSD can dramatically improve boot times, application loading times, and overall system responsiveness.

SSDs use flash memory to store data, which allows them to access data much faster than mechanical hard drives. SSDs are also more durable, quieter, and consume less power than mechanical hard drives.

To install an SSD, follow these steps:

1. **Choose the Right SSD:** Choose an SSD that is compatible with your laptop or computer. Consider the form factor (2.5-inch or M.2), the interface (SATA or NVMe), and the capacity.
2. **Back Up Your Data:** Back up all your important data before installing the SSD.
3. **Clone or Reinstall the Operating System:** You can either clone your existing hard drive to the SSD or perform a clean installation of the operating system. Cloning is faster, but a clean installation can resolve software problems and improve performance.
4. **Power Off and Disconnect:** Power off your computer and unplug it from the power outlet.
5. **Ground Yourself:** Use an anti-static wrist strap to prevent static electricity from damaging the components.
6. **Open the Case:** Open the computer case or the hard drive compartment on your laptop.
7. **Remove the Old Hard Drive:** Remove the old hard drive from its bay or bracket.
8. **Install the SSD:** Install the SSD into the hard drive bay or bracket.
9. **Connect the Cables:** Connect the SATA data and power cables to the SSD.
10. **Configure the BIOS/UEFI:** Configure the BIOS/UEFI to boot from the SSD.
11. **Close the Case:** Close the computer case or the hard drive compartment on your laptop.

Case Study: The SSD Upgrade That Saved a Laptop From the Landfill

A computer user was about to throw away their old laptop because it was too slow to use. A friend suggested that they try upgrading to an SSD before giving up on it.

The user installed a new SSD and performed a clean installation of the operating system. The results were dramatic. The laptop booted up in seconds, applications loaded instantly, and the overall system responsiveness was much improved. The user was able to continue using the laptop for several more years, saving them the cost of buying a new one.

Upgrading the RAM or storage can provide a significant boost in performance to your laptop or computer. By following these guidelines, you can perform these upgrades safely and effectively, breathing new life into your machine and extending its lifespan.

(7.4) Overheating Solutions: Cleaning and Thermal Paste

Overheating is a major enemy of laptops and computers, leading to performance slowdowns, system instability, and even permanent damage. While some overheating issues stem from demanding tasks or environmental factors, the most common culprits are a clogged cooling system and degraded thermal paste. Think of this section as your guide to breathing new life into your machine's cooling system, restoring its ability to dissipate heat and maintain optimal performance.

The Cooling System: A Vital Organ

The cooling system is responsible for dissipating the heat generated by the CPU, GPU, and other components. It typically consists of a heatsink, a fan, and vents that allow air to flow through the system. The heatsink is a metal block that is designed to absorb heat from the components and transfer it to the air. The fan helps to circulate air through the heatsink, carrying the heat away from the components.

Over time, the cooling system can become clogged with dust, pet hair, and other debris, which reduces its efficiency and causes the laptop or computer to overheat. Regular cleaning of the cooling system is essential for maintaining optimal performance and preventing damage.

Tools of the Trade: Essential Cleaning Supplies

To clean the cooling system, you'll need the following tools:

- **Compressed Air:** A can of compressed air is essential for blowing dust and debris out of the heatsink and fan.
- **Small Brush:** A small brush can be used to loosen stubborn dust and debris.
- **Screwdriver Set:** You'll need a screwdriver set to open the laptop or computer case and access the cooling system.
- **Anti-Static Wrist Strap:** Protects sensitive components from electrostatic discharge.

Cleaning the Cooling System: A Step-by-Step Guide

1. **Power Down and Disconnect:** Power off your computer and unplug it from the power outlet.
2. **Ground Yourself:** Use an anti-static wrist strap to prevent static electricity from damaging the components.
3. **Open the Case:** Open the computer case or the cooling system access panel on your laptop. Consult your system's repair guide to learn how to do this properly.
4. **Locate the Cooling System:** Locate the heatsink and fan.
5. **Blow Out the Dust:** Use compressed air to blow out the dust and debris from the heatsink and fan. Hold the can of compressed air upright and use short bursts to avoid damaging the components.
6. **Brush Away Stubborn Debris:** Use a small brush to loosen any stubborn dust and debris.
7. **Inspect the Vents:** Make sure that the vents on the laptop or computer case are not blocked.
8. **Reassemble:** Reassemble the laptop or computer.

The Thermal Paste Refresh: Optimizing Heat Transfer

Thermal paste is a substance that is applied between the CPU/GPU and the heatsink to improve heat transfer. Over time, thermal paste can dry out or degrade, reducing its effectiveness. Replacing the thermal paste can significantly improve the cooling performance.

Tools for Applying Thermal Paste

- **Isopropyl Alcohol:** Used to clean the old thermal paste from the CPU/GPU and heatsink.
- **Lint-Free Cloth or Coffee Filters:** For cleaning.
- **New Thermal Paste:** High-quality thermal paste is essential for effective heat transfer.
- **Spreader Card or Cotton Swab:** For applying the thermal paste.

Steps for Reapplying Thermal Paste

1. **Remove the Heatsink:** Carefully remove the heatsink from the CPU/GPU.
2. **Clean the Old Thermal Paste:** Use isopropyl alcohol and a lint-free cloth or coffee filter to clean the old thermal paste from the

CPU/GPU and heatsink. Make sure the surfaces are completely clean and dry.

3. **Apply New Thermal Paste:** Apply a small amount of new thermal paste to the center of the CPU/GPU. There are several methods for applying thermal paste, including the pea method, the line method, and the spread method. Choose the method that you are most comfortable with and that provides the best coverage for your CPU/GPU.

4. **Reinstall the Heatsink:** Carefully reinstall the heatsink onto the CPU/GPU. Make sure that the heatsink is properly seated and that the screws are tightened evenly.

Case Study: The Overclocked CPU Saved by a Thermal Paste Refresh

A computer enthusiast was overclocking their CPU to improve its performance. However, the CPU was overheating, even with a high-end cooler.

After doing some research, they decided to try reapplying the thermal paste. They carefully removed the old thermal paste and applied a new layer of high-quality thermal paste.

The results were dramatic. The CPU temperatures dropped significantly, allowing them to overclock the CPU even further without experiencing overheating problems. This illustrates how effective thermal paste can be at improving heat transfer.

Cleaning the cooling system and reapplying thermal paste are essential maintenance procedures for laptops and computers. By performing these tasks regularly, you can prevent overheating, improve performance, and extend the lifespan of your machine.

(7.5) Display Troubleshooting & Repair

A malfunctioning display can render a laptop or computer virtually useless. Whether it's a blank screen, distorted image, or flickering display, display problems can be frustrating and disruptive. This section provides a comprehensive guide to troubleshooting and resolving common display issues, empowering you to identify the root cause of the problem and restore your screen to its former glory. It's about illuminating the path to a clear and functional display.

Understanding the Landscape: Different Display Technologies

Before diving into troubleshooting, it's helpful to understand the different display technologies used in laptops and computers:

- **LCD (Liquid Crystal Display):** LCDs are the most common type of display used in laptops and desktop monitors. They use a backlight to illuminate a layer of liquid crystals, which are controlled by an electric field to create an image.
- **LED (Light Emitting Diode):** LEDs are used as the backlight source in many LCD displays. LED backlights are more energy-efficient and provide better color accuracy than traditional fluorescent backlights.
- **OLED (Organic Light Emitting Diode):** OLED displays are becoming increasingly popular in high-end laptops and smartphones. OLED displays do not require a backlight. Instead, each pixel emits its own light, resulting in richer colors, deeper blacks, and wider viewing angles.

Understanding the type of display used in your laptop or computer can help you narrow down the possible causes of display problems.

A Systematic Approach to Diagnosis: From Simple to Complex

Troubleshooting display problems requires a systematic approach, starting with the simplest and most common causes and working your way up to the more complex and less likely causes.

Step 1: External Connections and Power

The first step is to rule out any external connection problems.

- **Check the Monitor Cable:** Make sure the monitor cable is securely connected to the computer and the monitor. Try using a different cable to rule out a faulty cable.
- **Check the Power:** Make sure the monitor is powered on and that the power cable is securely connected.
- **Try a Different Monitor or Device:** If you have an external monitor, connect it to the computer to see if the problem is with the laptop screen or the graphics card. Or, connect the monitor to another computer to test.

Step 2: Driver Dilemmas

Graphics drivers are essential for proper display functionality. Outdated, corrupted, or incompatible drivers can cause a variety of display problems.

- **Update the Graphics Driver:** Make sure you have the latest graphics driver installed. You can download the latest drivers from the graphics card manufacturer's website (NVIDIA, AMD, or Intel).
- **Roll Back the Driver:** If you recently updated the graphics driver and started experiencing display problems, try rolling back to the previous driver version.

Step 3: The Backlight Mystery

If the screen is dark, but you can still faintly see an image, the backlight may have failed.

- **External Light Test:** In a darkened room, shine a flashlight at the screen at a low angle. Can you see faint images? If so, this is a good indication that the backlight is not working.
- **Inverter Test (LCD Only):** LCD screens use an inverter to supply power to the backlight. A faulty inverter can cause the backlight to fail. Replacing the inverter is a common repair for older LCD screens. This requires disassembly of the screen.

Step 4: Internal Investigations - Opening the Laptop

If the external connections, drivers, and backlight are all working properly, the problem may lie within the laptop itself.

- **Check the Internal Display Cable:** Open the laptop and check the display cable that connects the screen to the motherboard. Make sure the cable is securely connected and that there are no signs of damage.
- **Look for Physical Damage:** Inspect the LCD or LED panel for any signs of physical damage, such as cracks or breaks.

Step 5: Advanced Troubleshooting

The following will likely require a professional:

- **Test the Graphics Card:** The graphics card may be failing. Testing a graphics card typically requires specialized equipment and expertise.
- **Replace the LCD or LED Panel:** Replacing the LCD or LED panel is a complex and delicate repair that should be performed by a qualified technician.

Case Study: The Flickering Screen That Was Caused by a Loose Cable

A laptop user was experiencing a flickering screen. They tried updating the graphics driver, but the problem persisted.

After consulting a repair guide, they decided to open the laptop and inspect the display cable. They found that the cable was loose and not properly seated in its connector.

They carefully reconnected the cable, and the flickering screen disappeared. This case illustrates the importance of checking the internal connections when troubleshooting display problems.

Troubleshooting display problems requires a systematic approach and a basic understanding of display technologies. By following these steps, you can identify the root cause of many display issues and restore your screen to its former glory.

(7.6) Keyboard Replacement

A malfunctioning keyboard can severely hinder the usability of a laptop, making it difficult or impossible to type, communicate, or perform essential tasks. Whether it's a few sticky keys, a completely unresponsive keyboard, or damage from a spill, replacing the keyboard is often the most effective solution. While the process can vary depending on the laptop model, the core principles remain the same. This section will serve as your guide to navigating the world of laptop keyboard replacement, empowering you to restore the tactile input you rely on. It's about bringing the keys back to life.

Identifying the Problem: Is it *Really* the Keyboard?

Before embarking on a keyboard replacement, it's important to rule out other potential causes of keyboard problems:

- **Software Issues:** Sometimes, keyboard problems can be caused by software glitches or driver issues. Try restarting your computer, updating your keyboard driver, or running a virus scan to rule out these possibilities.
- **Sticky Keys Feature:** Make sure the "Sticky Keys" accessibility feature is not enabled. This feature can cause keys to behave erratically.
- **External Keyboard Test:** If possible, connect an external keyboard to the laptop to see if it works properly. If the external keyboard works, it confirms that the problem is with the laptop's keyboard.

Finding the Right Replacement: Compatibility is Key

The most crucial step in keyboard replacement is finding a compatible replacement keyboard for your laptop model. Keyboards are not universal, and using the wrong keyboard can damage your laptop or simply not work.

- **Model Number:** Start by identifying the exact model number of your laptop. This information can typically be found on a sticker on the bottom of the laptop or in the system information.
- **Part Number:** Look for the part number printed on the back of the original keyboard. This number will help you find an exact replacement.
- **Online Retailers:** Search online retailers for replacement keyboards that are compatible with your laptop model. Be sure to read reviews carefully before making a purchase.

Disassembly: Proceed with Caution

The keyboard replacement process varies greatly depending on the laptop model. Some laptops have keyboards that can be easily removed from the top, while others require disassembling the entire laptop.

Always consult a reputable repair guide for your specific laptop model before attempting to disassemble it. Websites like iFixit offer detailed, step-by-step instructions and photos.

Here are some general tips for disassembling a laptop to replace the keyboard:

- **Power Off and Disconnect:** Power off the laptop and disconnect it from the power outlet.
- **Remove the Battery:** Remove the battery to prevent accidental short circuits.
- **Locate the Keyboard Screws:** The keyboard may be secured by screws on the bottom of the laptop or under the battery compartment.
- **Use Plastic Opening Tools:** Use plastic opening tools to gently pry the keyboard loose from the case. Be careful not to damage the plastic.
- **Disconnect the Keyboard Cable:** The keyboard is connected to the motherboard by a ribbon cable. Gently disconnect the cable from the connector.

Installation: A Delicate Touch

Installing the new keyboard requires a delicate touch and careful attention to detail.

- **Connect the Keyboard Cable:** Carefully connect the new keyboard cable to the connector on the motherboard. Make sure the cable is fully seated and locked in place.
- **Position the Keyboard:** Position the new keyboard in the case, aligning it properly.
- **Secure the Keyboard:** Secure the keyboard with the screws or clips that were removed during disassembly.
- **Test the Keyboard:** Before fully reassembling the laptop, test the keyboard to make sure that all the keys are working properly.

Reassembly: Putting it All Back Together

Follow the disassembly instructions in reverse order to reassemble the laptop.

- **Make sure all cables are properly reconnected**
- **Tighten all screws securely**
- **Power On the Device to Test.**

Case Study: The Coffee Spill Catastrophe

A laptop user spilled coffee on their keyboard, causing several keys to stop working. They tried cleaning the keyboard, but the damage was irreversible.

They purchased a replacement keyboard online and followed a repair guide to disassemble the laptop and install the new keyboard. The replacement was a success, and the laptop was fully functional again.

Replacing a laptop keyboard can seem daunting, but with the right tools, a reliable repair guide, and a bit of patience, it's a repair that many users can perform at home. It's about taking control and giving new life to a vital component of your machine.

(7.7) Operating System Issues: Recovery & Reinstallation

While hardware failures often grab the spotlight, operating system (OS) issues are a frequent source of frustration for laptop and computer users. A corrupted OS can lead to slow performance, frequent crashes, startup problems, and a host of other problems. Fortunately, most operating systems offer built-in recovery tools that can often resolve these issues without the need for a complete reinstallation. And when recovery isn't enough, a clean OS installation can provide a fresh start and restore your machine to its former glory. Think of this section as your guide to navigating the often-complex world of OS recovery and reinstallation, empowering you to take control of your software and keep your machine running smoothly. It's about learning how to "reboot" your system's software soul.

Beyond the Hype: Is Reinstallation *Really* Necessary?

Before embarking on the potentially time-consuming process of reinstalling the operating system, it's important to consider whether other solutions might be more appropriate. Reinstallation should be reserved for situations where other troubleshooting steps have failed.

Many performance issues can be resolved by:

- **Removing Unnecessary Programs:** Uninstalling programs you no longer use can free up disk space and system resources.
- **Cleaning Up Startup Programs:** Disabling programs that run automatically at startup can speed up the boot process.
- **Running a Virus Scan:** Malware can cause a variety of performance problems. Running a virus scan can help identify and remove malicious software.
- **Updating Drivers:** Outdated drivers can cause compatibility issues and performance problems. Make sure all your drivers are up to date.

However, if you've tried these steps and are still experiencing problems, it may be time to consider OS recovery or reinstallation.

Recovery Options: Rolling Back to a Better Time

Most operating systems offer built-in recovery tools that allow you to revert your system to a previous state. These tools can be useful for resolving problems caused by recent software installations or configuration changes.

- **System Restore (Windows):** System Restore creates snapshots of your system files and settings at regular intervals. You can use System Restore to revert your computer to a previous snapshot, effectively undoing any changes that have caused problems.
- **Time Machine (macOS):** Time Machine is a backup utility that automatically backs up your entire system, including your files, applications, and settings. You can use Time Machine to restore your entire system to a previous point in time.

The Fresh Start: Performing a Clean Installation

When recovery options are not sufficient, a clean installation of the operating system may be necessary. This involves erasing the entire hard drive and reinstalling the OS from scratch. A clean installation can resolve a wide range of problems, including:

- **Severe Malware Infections:** A clean installation can completely remove stubborn malware that cannot be removed by antivirus software.

- **Corrupted System Files:** A clean installation can replace corrupted system files with fresh, uncorrupted copies.
- **Persistent Performance Problems:** A clean installation can provide a fresh start and resolve persistent performance problems.

To perform a clean installation, you'll need the following:

- **A Bootable USB Drive or DVD:** You'll need a bootable USB drive or DVD containing the operating system installation files. You can create a bootable USB drive using the Media Creation Tool (Windows) or by downloading the installation files from the Apple website (macOS).
- **Your Product Key (Windows):** If you're reinstalling Windows, you'll need your product key to activate the operating system.

The clean installation process typically involves booting from the USB drive or DVD, formatting the hard drive, and following the on-screen instructions to install the operating system.

Backing Up Your Data: A Critical Precaution

Before performing any OS recovery or reinstallation, it's essential to back up your important data. This will prevent you from losing your files, photos, documents, and other important information.

There are several ways to back up your data:

- **External Hard Drive:** Copy your files to an external hard drive.
- **Cloud Storage:** Upload your files to a cloud storage service, such as Google Drive, OneDrive, or Dropbox.
- **Backup Software:** Use backup software to create a complete image of your hard drive. This will allow you to restore your entire system, including your files, applications, and settings.

Case Study: The Computer Saved From Certain Doom

An IT professional was asked to perform a repair on a laptop for a client. The computer wouldn't even boot, and showed only a jumbled mess of error messages.

The user's data was backed up to an external hard drive, and a clean installation of Windows was performed. The IT professional then installed all the necessary drivers and applications and restored the user's data.

The laptop was as good as new, and the client was thrilled.

Addressing operating system issues can range from simple troubleshooting to a full reinstallation, but having a strategy, understanding the risks, and knowing the tools available can empower you to regain control of your system and restore it to optimal performance.

Chapter 8: Home Appliance Basics Repair

Welcome to Chapter 8, where we'll broaden our horizons beyond handheld devices and computers to explore the world of home appliance repair. From washing machines to refrigerators, our homes are filled with appliances that make our lives easier. When these appliances break down, it can be tempting to call a repair technician or simply buy a new one. However, many common appliance problems can be diagnosed and resolved with some basic knowledge and simple tools.

Important Note: Appliance repair can be dangerous, as it often involves working with high voltages and potentially hazardous components. **This chapter is intended to provide a basic introduction to appliance repair and is not a substitute for professional training or expertise. If you are not comfortable working with electricity or appliances, please consult a qualified technician.** Due to the increased safety concerns, this chapter will focus primarily on diagnostic techniques and very basic repairs that a handy DIYer can accomplish.

(8.1) Safety First: Working with Appliances

Unlike the relatively low-voltage world of smartphone or computer repair, working with home appliances introduces a new level of risk due to higher voltages, heavier components, and the potential for exposure to hazardous materials. It's easy to become complacent when working around the house, but even seemingly simple repairs can become dangerous if proper safety precautions are not followed. This section is not just a list of rules; it's a plea for your safety, designed to instill a deep respect for the potential hazards and to equip you with the knowledge to minimize those risks. Think of it as your pre-flight safety briefing before taking on any appliance repair task.

Understanding the Hazards: A Different Beast Altogether

The dangers associated with appliance repair are multifaceted:

- **High Voltage:** Many appliances operate on 120V or 240V AC power, which can deliver a lethal electrical shock. Even when the appliance is unplugged, some components, such as capacitors, can store a dangerous electrical charge.
- **Moving Parts:** Appliances often have moving parts, such as motors, belts, and gears, that can cause serious injuries if they are accidentally activated.
- **Heavy Components:** Appliances can be heavy and difficult to move, increasing the risk of strains, sprains, and other injuries.
- **Sharp Edges:** Appliances often have sharp edges and corners that can cause cuts and scrapes.
- **Hazardous Materials:** Some appliances contain hazardous materials, such as refrigerants, which can be harmful if inhaled or ingested.
- **Gas Lines:** Some appliances, like gas dryers, connect to gas lines, presenting a risk of explosion and asphyxiation.

Preparation is Key: More Than Just Unplugging

Before you even touch an appliance, thorough preparation is essential.

1. **Read the Manual:** Consult the appliance's owner's manual for safety information and specific instructions.
2. **Identify the Power Source:** Determine the power source for the appliance. Is it plugged into an electrical outlet? Is it hardwired to the electrical system? Is it connected to a gas line?
3. **Gather Your Tools:** Make sure you have all the necessary tools, including insulated screwdrivers, pliers, and wire strippers.
4. **Create a Safe Workspace:** Choose a well-lit and well-ventilated workspace. Clear away any clutter and make sure you have plenty of room to work.
5. **Tell Someone:** Make sure someone knows you're working on an appliance, and ensure they know what to do in an emergency.

The Safety Checklist: A Non-Negotiable Ritual

The following is a non-negotiable checklist of safety precautions that should be followed every time you work on an appliance:

- **Disconnect the Power:** The most important step is to disconnect the power from the appliance. For appliances that are plugged into an electrical outlet, unplug the power cord. For appliances that are hardwired to the electrical system, turn off the circuit breaker.

- **Discharge Capacitors:** Some appliances, such as microwave ovens and air conditioners, contain high-voltage capacitors that can store a dangerous electrical charge even after the power has been disconnected. Discharge these capacitors using a resistor and insulated tools before working on the appliance.
- **Lockout/Tagout:** If you are working on an appliance in a commercial or industrial setting, follow lockout/tagout procedures to prevent accidental activation of the appliance.
- **Test for Voltage:** Use a multimeter to test for voltage on any wires or components before touching them. Even after disconnecting the power, there may still be residual voltage present.
- **Use Insulated Tools:** Use insulated tools to prevent accidental contact with live circuits.
- **Wear Safety Glasses:** Wear safety glasses to protect your eyes from flying debris.
- **Wear Gloves:** Wear gloves to protect your hands from sharp edges, chemicals, and electrical shock.
- **Work in a Well-Ventilated Area:** Work in a well-ventilated area to avoid inhaling harmful fumes from refrigerants or other chemicals.
- **Avoid Working Alone:** If possible, have someone else present while you are working on an appliance in case of an emergency.
- **Check for Gas Leaks:** If working on a gas appliance, check for leaks.

Case Study: The Near Miss with a Microwave Capacitor

A homeowner decided to repair their microwave oven. They unplugged the microwave, but they did not discharge the high-voltage capacitor.

As they were working on the microwave, they accidentally touched the capacitor terminals with a metal screwdriver. The capacitor discharged with a loud bang, and the homeowner received a severe electrical shock. Fortunately, they were not seriously injured, but the incident served as a reminder of the dangers of working with high-voltage components.

Prioritizing safety when working with appliances is not just a matter of following a few rules; it's a matter of developing a safety-conscious mindset. By understanding the hazards, preparing thoroughly, and following the safety checklist every time, you can minimize the risk of accidents and enjoy the satisfaction of repairing your appliances safely and effectively. Always remember, your well-being is the top priority.

(8.2) Common Appliance Problems (Washing Machines, Dryers, Refrigerators - Basic)

Our homes are filled with appliances designed to make life easier, but when those appliances malfunction, life can quickly become more complicated. This section provides a concise overview of common problems you might encounter with washing machines, dryers, and refrigerators. Recognizing these symptoms and understanding potential causes can help you decide whether a simple DIY fix is possible or if it's time to call in a professional. This is about empowering you to be an informed homeowner, not necessarily a master appliance technician. Remember that safety always comes first.

Washing Machine Woes: When Clothes Don't Come Clean

Washing machines, with their complex interplay of water, electricity, and mechanical components, can experience a variety of issues:

- **Not Draining Properly:** This is often caused by a clogged drain pump, a kinked drain hose, or a faulty drain valve. Symptoms include water remaining in the drum after the wash cycle.
- **Not Spinning:** This may be due to a broken belt, a faulty motor, or a problem with the lid switch (which prevents the machine from spinning when the lid is open). Symptoms include wet clothes after the cycle is complete.
- **Leaking:** Leaks can come from various sources, including a worn-out door seal, a cracked hose, or a faulty water inlet valve. Symptoms include water pooling around the machine.
- **Not Filling with Water:** This may be caused by a faulty water inlet valve, a clogged water inlet screen, or a problem with the water pressure. Symptoms include the machine running but not filling with water.
- **Unusual Noises:** Banging, grinding, or squealing noises can indicate a variety of problems, such as worn-out bearings, a loose belt, or a foreign object in the drum.

Dryer Dilemmas: When Clothes Stay Damp

Dryers, despite their seemingly simple function, can also experience a range of problems that prevent them from effectively drying clothes:

- **Not Heating:** This is often caused by a faulty heating element (electric dryers), a faulty gas valve (gas dryers), or a tripped thermal fuse. Symptoms include clothes coming out damp after a full cycle.
- **Not Tumbling:** This may be due to a broken belt, a faulty motor, or a problem with the drum rollers. Symptoms include the drum not rotating during the cycle.
- **Taking Too Long to Dry:** This can be caused by a clogged lint trap, a blocked vent, or a faulty heating element. Symptoms include clothes taking an excessively long time to dry.
- **Unusual Noises:** Squealing, thumping, or grinding noises can indicate worn-out belts, rollers, or other mechanical problems.

Refrigerator Riddles: When Food Gets Warm

Refrigerators, with their sealed systems and complex temperature controls, often present more challenging diagnostic problems. This section will primarily focus on issues that do not require opening the sealed refrigerant system!

- **Not Cooling:** This can be caused by a faulty compressor, a blocked condenser coil, or a problem with the temperature control. Symptoms include the refrigerator not maintaining a cold temperature.
- **Leaking Water:** This may be due to a clogged defrost drain, a leaky door seal, or a frozen water line. Symptoms include water pooling inside or outside the refrigerator.
- **Making Strange Noises:** Humming, buzzing, or clicking noises can indicate a faulty compressor, a bad fan motor, or a problem with the defrost system.
- **Freezer Not Working:** If the refrigerator is cooling but the freezer is not, this may indicate a problem with the defrost system or the damper that controls airflow between the refrigerator and freezer compartments.
- **Ice Maker Malfunctions:** A faulty water line or jammed ice detector can prevent an ice maker from working.

Limitations of DIY: When to Call the Pros

It's important to recognize the limitations of DIY appliance repair. Some problems, such as those involving sealed refrigerant systems (refrigerators and air conditioners) or gas lines (gas dryers and ovens), should only be addressed by qualified professionals. Attempting to repair these systems without proper training and equipment can be dangerous and illegal.

This section is intended to provide you with a basic understanding of common appliance problems. The next sections will focus on identifying basic faulty components and performing simple repairs that can be safely undertaken by homeowners.

(8.3) Identifying Faulty Components (Fuses, Motors, Heating Elements - Basic)

Once you've identified a potential problem with your appliance, the next step is to pinpoint the faulty component. While complex electronic control boards require specialized diagnostic skills, there are a few basic components that can be tested relatively easily using a multimeter. This section provides a simplified guide to testing fuses, motors, and heating elements, empowering you to make informed decisions about whether to replace these components or seek professional assistance. Remember, safety is always paramount. This is about equipping yourself to identify the low-hanging fruit of appliance malfunctions.

The First Line of Defense: Testing Fuses

Fuses are safety devices designed to protect electrical circuits from overcurrents. When a circuit experiences an overload, the fuse blows, interrupting the flow of electricity and preventing damage to other components. A blown fuse is a common cause of appliance failures.

Visually inspecting a fuse can sometimes reveal whether it has blown. Look for a broken filament or a blackened glass enclosure. However, a visual inspection is not always reliable, so it's best to test the fuse with a multimeter.

To test a fuse, set the multimeter to the continuity setting (often indicated by a diode symbol or a sound wave symbol). Touch the probes to the two ends of the fuse.

- **Good Fuse:** If the fuse is good, the multimeter will beep or display a value close to zero ohms, indicating continuity.
- **Blown Fuse:** If the fuse is blown, the multimeter will not beep and will display "OL" (overload) or a very high resistance, indicating no continuity.

If you find a blown fuse, it's important to identify and correct the cause of the overcurrent before replacing the fuse. Replacing a blown fuse without addressing the underlying problem will likely result in the new fuse blowing as well. Common causes of blown fuses include short circuits, faulty components, and overloaded circuits.

Testing for Movement: Motors and Continuity

Motors are used to power various functions in appliances, such as the drum in a washing machine, the fan in a dryer, or the compressor in a refrigerator. A faulty motor can prevent the appliance from functioning properly.

Testing a motor typically involves checking for continuity and resistance in the motor windings.

1. **Disconnect the Power:** As always, disconnect the power from the appliance before testing the motor.
2. **Locate the Motor Terminals:** Locate the motor terminals. These are typically labeled with letters or numbers.
3. **Check for Continuity:** Set the multimeter to the continuity setting and touch the probes to the motor terminals. You should find continuity across at least two of the terminals. If there is no continuity between any of the terminals, the motor windings may be open.
4. **Check Resistance:** Use the multimeter to measure the resistance between each pair of motor terminals. The resistance values should be within a few ohms of each other. If the resistance is significantly different between any of the terminals, the motor windings may be shorted or damaged.

Generating Heat: Testing Heating Elements

Heating elements are used to generate heat in appliances, such as dryers, ovens, and water heaters. A faulty heating element can prevent the appliance from heating properly.

To test a heating element, follow these steps:

1. **Disconnect the Power:** As always, disconnect the power from the appliance before testing the heating element.
2. **Locate the Heating Element Terminals:** Locate the heating element terminals.
3. **Check for Continuity:** Set the multimeter to the continuity setting and touch the probes to the heating element terminals. You should find continuity. If there is no continuity, the heating element is likely open.
4. **Check Resistance:** Use the multimeter to measure the resistance of the heating element. The resistance value will vary depending on the wattage and voltage of the heating element. Consult the appliance's service manual or the heating element's specifications to determine the expected resistance value.

Case Study: The Dryer That Wouldn't Heat

A homeowner was experiencing problems with their electric dryer. The dryer was tumbling, but it was not heating.

They followed a repair guide and used a multimeter to test the heating element. The multimeter showed no continuity, indicating that the heating element was open.

They purchased a replacement heating element online and installed it in the dryer. The dryer started heating properly, and the homeowner saved the cost of calling a repair technician.

Identifying faulty components is a crucial step in appliance repair. By learning how to test fuses, motors, and heating elements with a multimeter, you can diagnose many common appliance problems and make informed decisions about whether to attempt a repair or seek professional assistance. Always remember to prioritize safety and to consult a qualified technician if you are not comfortable performing a particular repair.

(8.4) Basic Appliance Repair Techniques (Limited Scope - DIY Focus)

Now that you have a basic understanding of common appliance problems and how to identify faulty components, let's explore a few simple repair techniques that you can safely undertake at home. This section is intentionally limited in scope, focusing on repairs that do not involve working with high-voltage circuits, sealed refrigerant systems, or gas lines. These are the "gateway repairs" that can save you money and empower you to maintain your appliances. Remember to proceed with caution and consult a qualified technician if you are not comfortable with any of these procedures. Your safety is always the top priority.

The Quick Fix: Replacing a Blown Fuse

Replacing a blown fuse is often the simplest and most common appliance repair. When an appliance suddenly stops working, a blown fuse is often the culprit. Replacing the fuse can restore the appliance to its former glory.

1. **Safety First:** As always, disconnect the power from the appliance before performing any repairs.
2. **Locate the Fuse:** Locate the fuse. It is typically located in a fuse box or fuse holder on the back or inside of the appliance. Consult your appliance's owner's manual to find the location of the fuse.
3. **Identify the Fuse Type and Rating:** Identify the fuse type and rating. This information is typically printed on the fuse itself. Make sure to replace the blown fuse with a fuse of the same type and rating. Using a fuse with a higher rating can be dangerous and can damage the appliance.
4. **Remove the Blown Fuse:** Use a fuse puller or a small screwdriver to carefully remove the blown fuse from the fuse holder.
5. **Install the New Fuse:** Insert the new fuse into the fuse holder.
6. **Test the Appliance:** Reconnect the power to the appliance and test it to make sure that it is working properly.

The Breath of Fresh Air: Cleaning a Dryer Vent

A clogged dryer vent can significantly reduce the efficiency of your dryer, causing it to take longer to dry clothes and increasing the risk of a fire.

Cleaning the dryer vent is a simple maintenance task that can improve the performance and safety of your dryer.

1. **Safety First:** Disconnect the power from the dryer before performing any repairs.
2. **Locate the Dryer Vent:** Locate the dryer vent. It is typically located on the back of the dryer.
3. **Disconnect the Vent Hose:** Disconnect the vent hose from the dryer and from the outside vent.
4. **Clean the Vent Hose:** Use a dryer vent cleaning brush or a vacuum cleaner to remove any lint or debris from the vent hose.
5. **Clean the Dryer Vent:** Use a dryer vent cleaning brush or a vacuum cleaner to remove any lint or debris from the dryer vent opening.
6. **Reassemble:** Reconnect the vent hose to the dryer and to the outside vent.
7. **Test the Dryer:** Reconnect the power to the dryer and test it to make sure that it is working properly.

The Flow Restored: Replacing a Washing Machine Water Inlet Valve

If your washing machine is not filling with water, the problem may be a faulty water inlet valve. The water inlet valve controls the flow of water into the washing machine.

1. **Safety First:** Disconnect the power and water supply from the washing machine before performing any repairs.
2. **Access the Valve:** Depending on your machine's model, you may need to remove the top or back panel to access the water inlet valve. Consult your machine's repair manual to determine how to do this.
3. **Disconnect Hoses:** Disconnect the water hoses and electrical connections from the old valve, noting their positions for reassembly.
4. **Install the New Valve:** Connect the water hoses and electrical connections to the new valve, ensuring they are securely attached.
5. **Reassemble:** Reassemble the washing machine, following the disassembly steps in reverse.
6. **Test the Machine:** Reconnect the power and water supply, and test the machine to ensure it fills correctly.

Case Study: Simple Repairs Save the Day

A homeowner was having problems with their washing machine. The machine was not filling with water. They called a repair technician, who told them that it would cost several hundred dollars to repair the machine.

The homeowner decided to try to repair the machine themselves. They consulted a repair guide and found that the most likely cause of the problem was a faulty water inlet valve.

They purchased a replacement water inlet valve online for $20 and installed it in the washing machine. The washing machine started filling with water properly.

Replacing a blown fuse, cleaning a dryer vent, and replacing a water inlet valve are just a few of the basic appliance repair techniques that you can safely undertake at home.

Remember to always prioritize safety and to consult a qualified technician if you are not comfortable performing a particular repair.

Part III: Extending Lifespan & Promoting Sustainability

Chapter 9: Preventative Maintenance for Electronics

Welcome to Chapter 9, where we'll shift our focus from fixing problems to preventing them in the first place! Like a regular oil change for your car, preventative maintenance for your electronics can significantly extend their lifespan and keep them running smoothly. Taking a proactive approach to device care can save you time, money, and frustration in the long run. Think of this chapter as your guide to becoming a responsible and proactive electronics owner, ensuring that your devices stay in top condition for years to come.

(9.1) Cleaning Techniques: Keeping Devices Dust-Free

Dust, seemingly innocuous, is a pervasive threat to the health and longevity of our electronic devices. It's not merely a cosmetic issue; dust accumulation can lead to overheating, reduced performance, and even permanent damage. Think of dust as an insidious enemy silently infiltrating your devices, slowly suffocating their performance. This section will arm you with the knowledge and techniques to effectively combat dust, ensuring your electronics stay clean, cool, and operating at their best.

Why Dust is More Than Just a Nuisance: The Real Dangers

Dust poses several threats to electronic devices:

- **Overheating:** Dust acts as an insulator, trapping heat inside the device. This can lead to overheating, which can damage sensitive components and reduce performance.
- **Reduced Airflow:** Dust can clog vents and fans, restricting airflow and preventing the cooling system from working properly.
- **Short Circuits:** Dust can conduct electricity, potentially causing short circuits and damaging components.
- **Reduced Lifespan:** Over time, accumulated dust can contribute to the premature failure of electronic components.

Regular cleaning is essential for preventing these problems and extending the lifespan of your devices.

The Right Tools for the Job: Avoiding Damage During Cleaning

Using the wrong cleaning tools can damage your electronic devices. Avoid using harsh chemicals, abrasive cleaners, or anything that could scratch the screen or damage the finish. Here are some essential cleaning tools:

- **Soft, Lint-Free Cloths:** Microfiber cloths are ideal for cleaning screens and other delicate surfaces.
- **Canned Compressed Air:** Essential for blowing dust and debris out of hard-to-reach areas, such as keyboards and ports.
- **Small Brushes:** Soft-bristled brushes can be used to loosen stubborn dust and debris.
- **Isopropyl Alcohol:** Use isopropyl alcohol (90% or higher) to clean stubborn dirt and grime. Be sure to apply the alcohol to a cloth, not directly to the device.
- **Cotton Swabs:** Useful for cleaning small areas and tight spaces.
- **Screen Cleaning Solution:** There are cleaning solutions specifically designed for use with electronic screens.

Cleaning Strategies: A Device-Specific Approach

The best cleaning techniques vary depending on the type of device you are cleaning.

- **Smartphones and Tablets:**
  - Power off the device.
  - Use a soft, lint-free cloth to wipe down the screen and back.
  - Use a cotton swab dipped in isopropyl alcohol to clean the charging port and other ports.
  - Avoid spraying liquids directly onto the device.
- **Laptops:**
  - Power off the laptop and disconnect it from the power outlet.
  - Use a soft, lint-free cloth to wipe down the screen, keyboard, and trackpad.
  - Use a can of compressed air to blow out the dust from the keyboard, vents, and ports.

- Use a cotton swab dipped in isopropyl alcohol to clean the ports.
- Consider opening the laptop to clean the internal components, as described in Chapter 7.
- **Desktop Computers:**
  - Power off the computer and disconnect it from the power outlet.
  - Use a soft, lint-free cloth to wipe down the case and monitor.
  - Use a can of compressed air to blow out the dust from the keyboard, vents, and ports.
  - Consider opening the computer case to clean the internal components, as described in Chapter 7.

A Word of Caution: Avoiding Common Mistakes

- **Never Use Abrasive Cleaners:** Abrasive cleaners can scratch screens and damage finishes.
- **Don't Spray Liquids Directly:** Never spray liquids directly onto electronic devices. Always apply the liquid to a cloth first.
- **Avoid Excessive Moisture:** Too much moisture can damage electronic components.
- **Be Gentle:** Use gentle pressure when cleaning. Applying too much pressure can damage the screen or other components.

Case Study: The Overheating Computer Saved by a Simple Cleaning

A computer user was experiencing frequent system crashes. The computer was also running very slowly.

After doing some research, they suspected that the computer was overheating. They decided to try cleaning the internal components.

They carefully opened the computer case and used a can of compressed air to blow out the dust from the heatsink and fan. They were amazed at how much dust had accumulated inside.

After cleaning the computer, the system crashes stopped, and the computer ran much faster. This case illustrates the importance of regular cleaning.

Keeping your electronic devices dust-free is an essential part of preventative maintenance. By following these tips, you can protect your devices from damage, improve their performance, and extend their lifespan.

(9.2) Protecting Your Devices: Cases, Screen Protectors, Surge Protectors

We rely on our electronic devices every day, often taking them for granted until something goes wrong. Protecting these investments from physical damage, scratches, and power surges is a key aspect of preventative maintenance. Think of cases, screen protectors, and surge protectors as your device's personal bodyguard, shielding it from the hazards of daily life. This section will guide you through the world of device protection, helping you choose the right armor for your precious electronics.

The First Line of Defense: Cases – Absorbing the Impact

A case provides a crucial layer of protection against drops, bumps, and scratches. Cases are available for a wide range of devices, including smartphones, tablets, laptops, and even some portable gaming consoles.

When choosing a case, consider the following factors:

- **Device Compatibility:** Make sure the case is specifically designed for your device model.
- **Protection Level:** Cases range from slim, minimalist designs to rugged, heavy-duty models. Choose a case that provides the level of protection you need based on your lifestyle and usage habits.
- **Material:** Cases are typically made from plastic, silicone, rubber, or a combination of materials. Each material offers different levels of protection and durability.
- **Features:** Some cases offer additional features, such as a built-in stand, a wallet, or a keyboard.
- **Aesthetics:** Choose a case that you like the look of. You're more likely to use a case if you find it visually appealing.

Shielding the Window: Screen Protectors - Preventing Scratches and Cracks

A screen protector is a thin sheet of transparent material that is applied to the screen of your device to protect it from scratches, scuffs, and even cracks.

- **Types of Screen Protectors:**
  - **Tempered Glass:** The strongest and most scratch-resistant.
  - **PET Plastic:** Offers scratch protection and a smooth feel.
  - **TPU (Thermoplastic Polyurethane):** Flexible and offers moderate impact protection.

Applying a screen protector can be tricky, but there are several tips to make the process easier:

- **Clean the Screen Thoroughly:** Use a microfiber cloth and a screen cleaning solution to remove any dust, fingerprints, or smudges from the screen.
- **Align the Protector Carefully:** Carefully align the screen protector with the screen before applying it.
- **Apply Pressure Evenly:** Apply pressure evenly across the screen protector to avoid air bubbles.
- **Use a Squeegee:** Use a squeegee or credit card to smooth out any air bubbles.

Guarding Against Power Surges: Surge Protectors – A Shield for Your Electronics

Power surges are sudden spikes in voltage that can damage electronic components. They can be caused by lightning strikes, power outages, or problems with the electrical grid. A surge protector is a device that protects electronic devices from power surges by diverting excess voltage to the ground.

- **Joules Rating:** The joules rating indicates the amount of energy the surge protector can absorb. Choose a surge protector with a high joules rating for better protection.
- **Number of Outlets:** Choose a surge protector with enough outlets to accommodate all of your devices.
- **Features:** Some surge protectors offer additional features, such as EMI/RFI filtering, which can reduce noise and interference on your electrical lines.
- **Warranty:** Choose a surge protector with a good warranty.

Case Study: The Lightning Strike That Saved Thousands

A small business owner had invested heavily in computer equipment, including several desktop computers, laptops, and servers. They had not invested in surge protectors, believing that they were not necessary.

One day, a lightning strike hit the building, causing a power surge that damaged all of their electronic equipment. The business owner lost thousands of dollars in equipment and data.

This case illustrates the importance of using surge protectors. A relatively small investment in surge protection could have saved the business owner a significant amount of money and data.

Protecting your electronic devices is an essential part of responsible ownership. By using cases, screen protectors, and surge protectors, you can significantly extend the lifespan of your devices and prevent costly repairs or replacements. It's about being proactive and investing in the long-term health of your electronic companions.

(9.3) Optimizing Software: Updates and Performance Tweaks

While physical protection safeguards your devices from the outside world, software optimization protects them from internal gremlins that can slow them down, compromise their security, and reduce their overall lifespan. Just like a well-tuned engine runs smoother and lasts longer, a well-maintained software environment keeps your devices performing at their best. This section is about becoming a software steward, ensuring your devices are running efficiently and securely. Think of it as giving your device a regular software check-up and tune-up.

The Power of Updates: Keeping Your System Secure and Efficient

Installing software updates is one of the most important steps you can take to protect your devices and improve their performance. Software updates often include:

- **Security Patches:** Security patches fix vulnerabilities that could be exploited by malware or hackers.

- **Bug Fixes:** Bug fixes resolve errors and glitches that can cause system crashes, performance problems, or other issues.
- **Performance Improvements:** Software updates can include optimizations that improve the speed and efficiency of the operating system and applications.
- **New Features:** Software updates may add new features and functionality to your devices.

Most operating systems and applications offer automatic updates, which can be configured to install updates automatically in the background. It's highly recommended that you enable automatic updates to ensure that your devices are always protected with the latest security patches.

Spring Cleaning for Your System: Removing the Digital Clutter

Over time, your computer can accumulate a lot of digital clutter, including temporary files, unnecessary programs, and old data. This clutter can consume system resources and slow down your computer.

Performing regular system cleanup can help to improve performance and free up disk space.

Here are some steps you can take to clean up your system:

- **Uninstall Unnecessary Programs:** Uninstall programs that you no longer use. This will free up disk space and prevent unnecessary programs from consuming system resources.
- **Remove Temporary Files:** Temporary files are created by programs and the operating system to store data temporarily. These files can accumulate over time and take up a significant amount of disk space. You can use the Disk Cleanup utility (Windows) or CleanMyMac (macOS) to remove temporary files.
- **Clean Up Your Downloads Folder:** Your downloads folder can quickly become cluttered with files that you no longer need. Take some time to review your downloads folder and delete any unnecessary files.
- **Empty the Recycle Bin/Trash:** Don't forget to empty the recycle bin (Windows) or trash (macOS) to permanently delete files that you have removed from your system.

Resource Management: Optimizing Your System Settings

Optimizing your system settings can also improve performance and extend the life of your devices.

- **Disable Startup Programs:** Programs that run automatically at startup can consume system resources and slow down the boot process. Disable any unnecessary startup programs to speed up the boot process.
- **Disable Visual Effects:** Disabling visual effects, such as animations and transparency, can improve performance on older or less powerful computers.
- **Adjust Power Settings:** Adjust the power settings to optimize battery life or performance. For example, you can set the computer to automatically turn off the display after a certain period of inactivity.
- **Defragment Your Hard Drive (HDDs Only):** Defragmenting your hard drive can improve performance by organizing the files on the drive. This is only necessary for traditional mechanical hard drives (HDDs), not solid-state drives (SSDs).

Case Study: The Performance Boost from a Driver Update

A gamer was experiencing poor performance in a new video game. The game was running slowly and frequently stuttering.

They checked the game's system requirements and confirmed that their computer met the minimum requirements. They tried adjusting the game's graphics settings, but the performance did not improve.

After doing some research, they discovered that their graphics driver was outdated. They downloaded and installed the latest graphics driver from the graphics card manufacturer's website.

The performance of the game improved dramatically. The game ran smoothly and without stuttering. This case illustrates the importance of keeping your drivers up to date.

Optimizing your software is an essential part of preventative maintenance for electronics. By following these tips, you can improve the performance, security, and lifespan of your devices.

(9.4) Battery Care: Maximizing Battery Life

In our mobile-centric world, battery life is a precious commodity. Whether it's your smartphone, laptop, or tablet, running out of battery power at a crucial moment can be incredibly frustrating. This section is your comprehensive guide to understanding battery technology and implementing best practices for maximizing battery life and maintaining the long-term health of your batteries. It's about becoming a battery whisperer, understanding your device's power needs and optimizing its performance for extended use.

Understanding the Enemy: Lithium-Ion Batteries and Their Quirks

Most modern laptops, smartphones, and tablets use lithium-ion (Li-ion) batteries. Li-ion batteries offer several advantages over older battery technologies, such as higher energy density, lower self-discharge, and no memory effect. However, they also have some limitations that must be understood to maximize their lifespan:

- **Degradation Over Time:** Li-ion batteries degrade over time, losing their capacity to hold a charge. This degradation is accelerated by heat, overcharging, and deep discharging.
- **Limited Charge Cycles:** Li-ion batteries have a limited number of charge cycles. A charge cycle is defined as fully charging and discharging the battery. After a certain number of charge cycles, the battery's capacity will significantly decrease.
- **Sensitivity to Temperature:** Extreme temperatures can damage Li-ion batteries and reduce their lifespan.
- **Voltage Sensitivity:** Li-ion batteries operate within a specific voltage range. Overcharging or deep discharging can damage the battery.

Best Practices for Maximizing Battery Life: The Golden Rules

To maximize battery life and maintain battery health, follow these best practices:

- **Avoid Extreme Temperatures:** Avoid exposing your devices to extreme temperatures. Do not leave your devices in direct sunlight or in a hot car.

- **Avoid Overcharging:** Avoid leaving your devices plugged in after they are fully charged. While modern devices have charging circuitry to prevent overcharging, prolonged exposure to full charge can still degrade the battery over time. Unplugging the device after a full charge is good practice.
- **Partial Charging is Okay (and Sometimes Better):** Unlike older battery technologies, Li-ion batteries do not need to be fully discharged before being recharged. In fact, partial charging is often better for the battery than full charging. It is better to keep the battery charge between 20% and 80% for the majority of the time.
- **Optimize Display Settings:** Reduce the screen brightness, shorten the screen timeout duration, and disable auto-brightness. The display is one of the biggest power consumers on most devices.
- **Disable Unnecessary Features:** Disable features that you are not using, such as Wi-Fi, Bluetooth, GPS, and location services.
- **Close Unused Apps:** Close apps that are running in the background but are not being used. These apps can consume system resources and drain the battery.
- **Use Power Saving Mode:** Most operating systems offer a power-saving mode that can extend battery life by reducing performance and limiting background activity.
- **Keep Software Updated:** Software updates often include battery optimization features.
- **Store Properly When Not in Use:** If you are not going to use a device for an extended period of time, store it with a partially charged battery (around 50%) in a cool, dry place.

The Myth of "Conditioning" New Batteries

In the past, it was necessary to "condition" new batteries by fully charging and discharging them several times to maximize their capacity. This is not necessary with modern Li-ion batteries. In fact, conditioning Li-ion batteries can actually be harmful.

Case Study: The Phone Saved by a Strategic Charge

A frequent traveler relies heavily on their smartphone for navigation and communication. They know they will be without access to charging for a long period. They avoid watching streaming videos or playing games to preserve as much battery as possible. They dim the screen, enable power saving mode, and strategically charge their phone in short bursts whenever a charging opportunity presents itself. By carefully managing their battery usage, they are able to keep their phone running for the entire trip.

Taking care of your batteries is essential for maximizing their lifespan and ensuring that your devices are always ready when you need them. By following these best practices, you can extend the life of your batteries and enjoy longer battery life on your laptops, smartphones, and tablets.

Chapter 10: Upgrading and Modifying Your Devices

Welcome to Chapter 10, where we'll explore the exciting world of upgrading and modifying your electronic devices! While repair focuses on restoring functionality, upgrading and modifying take it a step further, enhancing performance, personalizing aesthetics, or adding new features. This chapter is designed to be your guide to transforming your devices, but with a strong emphasis on responsible modification and ethical considerations. It's about unlocking the hidden potential of your electronics while staying within safe and ethical boundaries.

(10.1) Performance Upgrades: RAM, SSDs, etc.

Is your laptop or computer feeling sluggish and struggling to keep up with your demands? Performance upgrades, particularly upgrading the RAM (Random Access Memory) and storage drive (typically to a Solid State Drive or SSD), are often the most cost-effective ways to breathe new life into an aging system or unlock the full potential of a more recent machine. It's like giving your device a shot of adrenaline, boosting its ability to handle demanding tasks and respond quickly. This section serves as your guide to understanding these upgrades, ensuring you make the right choices for your specific needs and budget.

RAM: The Key to Smooth Multitasking

RAM acts as your computer's short-term memory, holding the data and instructions that the CPU is actively using. When you run multiple programs simultaneously or work with large files, your computer relies heavily on RAM. Insufficient RAM can lead to slow performance, frequent freezing, and frustrating delays.

Think of RAM as your desk space. The more desk space you have, the more papers and projects you can have open at the same time without feeling cramped and disorganized. Similarly, the more RAM you have, the more programs you can run simultaneously without experiencing performance slowdowns.

Upgrading the RAM is generally one of the simplest and most impactful performance upgrades you can make, especially for older systems with limited RAM.

However, before rushing out to buy more RAM, it's important to consider the following:

- **Compatibility:** Not all RAM is created equal. Different laptops and computers use different types of RAM, such as DDR3, DDR4, and DDR5. Consult your computer's documentation or use a tool like CPU-Z to determine the correct type of RAM for your system.
- **Maximum Capacity:** Your laptop or computer has a maximum amount of RAM that it can support. Check your computer's documentation or the motherboard manufacturer's website to determine the maximum capacity.
- **Number of Slots:** Determine the number of RAM slots available in your laptop or computer. Some laptops have only one RAM slot, while others have two or more.
- **Speed:** RAM is rated by its speed, measured in MHz. While faster RAM can improve performance, it's important to choose RAM that is compatible with your system. Check your computer's documentation to determine the supported RAM speeds.

SSDs: The Storage Revolution

Traditional mechanical hard drives (HDDs) have been the standard storage device in computers for decades. However, solid-state drives (SSDs) have revolutionized storage technology, offering significantly faster performance, greater durability, and lower power consumption.

Replacing a traditional hard drive with an SSD can dramatically improve boot times, application loading times, file transfer speeds, and overall system responsiveness. The difference is so significant that it often feels like you've purchased an entirely new computer.

Think of an HDD as reading from a record player, where a physical arm and needle must move to locate the data. SSDs, on the other hand, are like reading from a flash drive, where data can be accessed almost instantly.

SSDs come in various form factors and interfaces:

- **2.5-inch SATA:** These SSDs are the same size and shape as traditional laptop hard drives and use the SATA interface. They are easy to install and compatible with most laptops and computers.
- **M.2 SATA:** These SSDs are smaller than 2.5-inch SSDs and plug directly into an M.2 slot on the motherboard. They offer similar performance to 2.5-inch SATA SSDs.
- **M.2 NVMe:** These SSDs are the fastest type of SSD and use the NVMe (Non-Volatile Memory Express) interface. They offer significantly faster performance than SATA SSDs. However, they require a motherboard with an M.2 NVMe slot.

When choosing an SSD, consider the following:

- **Capacity:** Choose a capacity that is large enough to accommodate your operating system, applications, and data.
- **Form Factor and Interface:** Make sure the SSD is compatible with your laptop or computer.
- **Performance:** Look for an SSD with fast read and write speeds.
- **Reliability:** Choose an SSD from a reputable brand with a good warranty.

Other Performance Enhancers:

- **Graphics Card (Desktops):** If you are a gamer or work with graphics-intensive applications, upgrading your graphics card can provide a significant performance boost.
- **CPU (Processors):** In some cases, upgrading the CPU can improve performance. However, this is often more complex and expensive than upgrading the RAM or storage.

Case Study: The Performance Upgrade That Doubled Productivity

A graphic designer was struggling to work on large image files with their aging laptop. The laptop was constantly freezing, and tasks that used to take minutes now took hours.

They upgraded the laptop's RAM from 8GB to 16GB and replaced the traditional hard drive with an SSD. The results were dramatic. The laptop booted up in seconds, applications loaded instantly, and they were able to work on large image files without experiencing any performance problems. Their productivity doubled, and they were able to complete projects in half the time.

Performance upgrades, such as upgrading the RAM and storage, can breathe new life into your laptop or computer, improving its speed, responsiveness, and overall usability. By carefully considering your needs and following these guidelines, you can choose the right upgrades for your system and unlock its full potential.

(10.2) Cosmetic Modifications: Personalizing Your Devices

While performance upgrades focus on what your devices *can do*, cosmetic modifications focus on how your devices *look*. In a world of mass-produced electronics, personalization allows you to express your individual style and make your devices truly unique. This section serves as your creative guide to transforming the aesthetics of your electronics, from subtle enhancements to bold transformations, all while keeping in mind the importance of responsible modification. It's about turning your device into a reflection of your personality.

Beyond Function: The Power of Personalization

Cosmetic modifications aren't just about making your devices look pretty; they can also enhance your user experience and even protect your devices from wear and tear. A custom phone case can provide better grip and protect against drops, while a keyboard skin can prevent keys from wearing out. Personalization is about making your devices both functional and visually appealing.

A Canvas for Creativity: Exploring the Options

There are countless ways to cosmetically modify your electronic devices. Here are some popular options:

- **Skins and Wraps:** Skins and wraps are vinyl decals that adhere to the exterior of your devices, providing a protective layer and allowing you to change their color, add patterns, or display custom designs. They are relatively inexpensive and easy to apply and remove.

- **Custom Cases:** Custom cases offer a more robust form of protection and personalization. Cases are available in a wide variety of materials, colors, and designs. You can even create your own custom cases using online design tools.
- **Stickers and Decals:** Vinyl stickers provide a simple and affordable way to add personality to your devices. You can find stickers featuring your favorite characters, logos, or designs.
- **Keyboard Skins:** Keyboard skins are silicone or TPU covers that fit over the keys of your laptop or computer keyboard. They protect the keys from wear and tear and can also change the look and feel of the keyboard.
- **Custom Keycaps:** Replacing the keycaps on your keyboard can personalize its appearance and improve the typing experience. Custom keycaps are available in a wide variety of materials, colors, and profiles.
- **Paint and Hydrographics:** More advanced modifications, like painting or hydrographics, offer greater levels of customization but require more skill and caution.
- **RGB Lighting:** Adding RGB lighting to your computer case can create a visually stunning effect. RGB lighting allows you to customize the color and pattern of the lights to match your personal style.
- **Cable Management:** Neatly organizing the cables in your computer can improve airflow and enhance the overall appearance of the system.

Responsible Modification: Avoiding Damage and Compromise

When making cosmetic modifications, it's important to proceed with caution and to avoid damaging your devices. Here are some tips for responsible modification:

- **Research Thoroughly:** Before making any modifications, research the process carefully and make sure you understand the risks involved.
- **Use the Right Tools:** Use the right tools for the job. This will help you avoid damaging your devices.
- **Proceed Slowly and Carefully:** Take your time and be careful not to force anything.
- **Avoid Harsh Chemicals:** Avoid using harsh chemicals or abrasive cleaners, as these can damage the finish of your devices.

- **Protect Vents and Sensors:** Be careful not to cover any important vents or sensors. This can cause your devices to overheat or malfunction.
- **Consider Resale Value:** Some modifications can decrease the resale value of your devices. Keep this in mind before making any irreversible changes.

Case Study: The Gamer's Rig - A Transformation

A gamer wanted to personalize their gaming PC to reflect their unique style and create a more immersive gaming experience.

They started by adding RGB lighting to the computer case. They then replaced the stock CPU cooler with a liquid cooler with RGB lighting.

Next, they installed custom keycaps on their mechanical keyboard. They also added a custom mousepad and headset stand.

Finally, they organized the cables inside the computer case, creating a clean and visually appealing interior.

The result was a stunning gaming rig that reflected their personal style and enhanced their gaming experience.

Cosmetic modifications can transform the appearance of your electronic devices and make them truly unique. By following these guidelines and exercising caution, you can personalize your devices without damaging them or compromising their functionality.

(10.3) Ethical Considerations: Warranty and Safety

While upgrading and modifying your devices can be a fun and rewarding experience, it's essential to consider the potential ethical implications and safety concerns. Modifying your devices can have consequences that extend beyond your personal enjoyment, impacting warranties, safety, and even the environment. This section is dedicated to providing a balanced perspective, urging you to proceed with awareness and responsibility. It's about understanding that with the power to modify comes the responsibility to do so ethically and safely.

The Warranty Void: A Costly Oversight

One of the most common consequences of modifying electronic devices is voiding the warranty. Most manufacturers have warranty terms and conditions that explicitly state that any unauthorized modifications will void the warranty. This means that if you damage your device during a modification or if the modification causes your device to malfunction, the manufacturer will not be responsible for repairing or replacing it.

Before making any modifications, carefully review the warranty terms and conditions for your device. If you are concerned about voiding the warranty, consider waiting until the warranty has expired before making any modifications. Also, be aware that some modifications are more likely to void the warranty than others. For example, opening the device case or replacing internal components is more likely to void the warranty than simply applying a skin or wrap.

Safety First: Avoiding Potential Hazards

Modifying electronic devices can also create safety hazards if not done properly.

- **Electrical Shock:** Working with electrical components can be dangerous if you are not familiar with basic electrical safety precautions. Always disconnect the power from the device before making any modifications.
- **Overheating:** Some modifications, such as overclocking a CPU or GPU, can cause the device to overheat. Overheating can damage components and even cause a fire. Make sure to use proper cooling solutions and to monitor the temperature of your device closely.
- **Battery Damage:** Damaging the battery can create a fire hazard. Only use approved batteries.
- **Component Damage:** Carelessly disassembling devices or forcing components can cause irreversible damage.

Environmental Responsibility: Thinking Beyond the Device

Our modifications and upgrades have an impact on the environment. Consider:

- **Responsible Disposal of Old Parts:** Don't just throw away old parts! Dispose of them properly through e-waste recycling programs.

- **Energy Consumption:** Upgrades can sometimes increase power consumption. Be mindful of energy efficiency when choosing new components.
- **Lifespan Extension:** While modifications can be fun, remember the goal of sustainable repair: extending the lifespan of existing devices.

Respecting Intellectual Property: Avoiding Infringement

When making modifications, it's important to respect the intellectual property rights of others. Avoid using copyrighted images or designs without permission. Also, avoid making modifications that infringe on patents or trademarks.

Case Study: The Overclocked CPU That Melted Down

A computer enthusiast was overclocking their CPU to improve its gaming performance. They pushed the CPU to its limits, but they did not use a proper cooling solution.

The CPU overheated and eventually melted down, damaging the motherboard and other components. The enthusiast had voided the warranty and caused significant damage to their computer.

This case illustrates the importance of following safety precautions and respecting the limitations of your hardware.

Modifying your electronic devices can be a rewarding experience, but it's important to consider the ethical implications and safety concerns. By following these guidelines and exercising caution, you can enhance your devices while staying within safe and responsible boundaries. Make sure you ask the question, "Am I putting safety and ethical considerations first?"

Chapter 11: The Power of Reuse & Responsible Recycling

Welcome to Chapter 11, where we'll explore what happens to our electronics when we're done with them. While previous chapters focused on repair and modification, this chapter focuses on responsible end-of-life decisions. The goal isn't just about fixing things; it's about creating a sustainable cycle where electronics are valued, reused, and ultimately recycled in an environmentally responsible manner. It's about shifting our mindset from disposable consumption to a more circular economy for electronics. Think of this as your guide to becoming an e-waste warrior, fighting for a more sustainable future.

(11.1) Extending Device Lifespan Through Repair

Throughout this book, we've emphasized the practical aspects of electronics repair: how to diagnose problems, replace components, and troubleshoot various issues. Now, let's step back and examine the bigger picture: the profound impact of extending device lifespan through repair. It's about understanding that choosing to repair isn't just a fix; it's a statement – a commitment to sustainability, resourcefulness, and a more responsible relationship with technology. Repair isn't merely a reaction to breakage; it's a proactive step towards a more sustainable future.

Beyond the Quick Fix: The Ripple Effects of Repair

Extending the lifespan of our electronic devices through repair generates a cascade of positive effects that ripple outwards, impacting our wallets, our environment, and our sense of self-reliance. It's a choice with far-reaching consequences.

- **Economic Benefits: Saving Money and Creating Value**

The most immediate benefit of repair is the direct cost savings. Repairing a broken device is almost always cheaper than buying a new one. But the economic benefits extend far beyond the initial savings. By extending the lifespan of our devices, we delay the need for replacement, which saves us money in the long run. Furthermore, repaired devices often retain a higher resale value than broken or neglected ones, creating an opportunity to recoup some of your investment.

Repair also stimulates local economies. Supporting independent repair shops keeps money in the community and creates jobs for skilled technicians. This contrasts with a model that funnels profits to large corporations and often outsources manufacturing and repair jobs overseas.

- **Environmental Benefits: Reducing E-Waste and Conserving Resources**

The environmental impact of electronics manufacturing and disposal is significant, as we discussed in Chapter 1. Repair plays a crucial role in reducing e-waste, conserving resources, and minimizing pollution.

By repairing our devices, we keep them out of landfills, where they can leach harmful toxins into the environment. We also reduce the demand for new electronics, which requires the extraction of raw materials, the consumption of energy, and the use of hazardous chemicals. Every repair is a small victory for the planet.

- **Personal Empowerment: Taking Control of Your Technology**

Repairing our own devices empowers us to become more informed and engaged consumers. We gain a deeper understanding of how our devices work, what their common failure points are, and how to maintain them properly. This knowledge not only saves us money but also gives us a greater sense of control over our technology.

Repairing your own electronics can also be a rewarding and empowering experience. It's a chance to learn new skills, challenge yourself, and take pride in your ability to fix things.

Overcoming the Obstacles: Embracing Repair in a Culture of Consumption

Despite the many benefits of repair, it's often seen as a less convenient or less desirable option than simply buying a new device. This is due to several factors:

- **Planned Obsolescence:** Many manufacturers design their products to become obsolete after a certain period of time, encouraging consumers to upgrade to the latest model.
- **Lack of Repair Information:** Manufacturers often make it difficult or impossible for consumers and independent repair shops to access the parts, tools, and information needed to repair their products.
- **Convenience of Replacement:** In today's fast-paced world, it's often easier and more convenient to simply buy a new device than to take the time to repair an old one.

To overcome these obstacles, we need to shift our mindset and embrace a culture of repair. This involves valuing the skills and knowledge of repair technicians, supporting the Right to Repair movement, and making informed purchasing decisions that prioritize durability and repairability.

Case Study: The Town That Embraced Repair

In a small town struggling with economic hardship, a group of residents decided to organize a repair cafe. The repair cafe was a community event where people could bring their broken appliances, electronics, and other items to be repaired by volunteer technicians.

The repair cafe was a huge success. Not only did it save residents money, but it also created a sense of community and fostered a culture of repair. The town's residents learned new skills, shared their knowledge with others, and reduced the amount of waste going to the local landfill.

Extending device lifespan through repair is not just a practical solution; it's a powerful act of sustainability, empowerment, and community building. By embracing repair, we can create a more responsible and resilient relationship with technology and contribute to a more sustainable future for all.

(11.2) Donating or Selling Used Electronics

Once you've maximized the lifespan of your devices through repair and maintenance, there comes a time when they no longer meet your needs. Perhaps you've upgraded to a newer model, or maybe the device is simply too old to run the latest software. Before relegating these devices to the e-waste pile, consider the powerful option of giving them a second life through donation or sale. It's about understanding that your "old" electronics can be a valuable resource for others, extending their usefulness and preventing them from becoming environmental burdens. This section is dedicated to guiding you through the process of responsibly giving your used electronics a new purpose.

The Value of a Second Life: Extending the Circle of Use

Donating or selling used electronics is a win-win situation for everyone involved. It benefits you by decluttering your home and potentially recouping some of your investment. It benefits the recipient by providing them with access to affordable technology. And it benefits the environment by reducing e-waste and conserving resources.

Donating to Charities: Giving Back and Making a Difference

Donating used electronics to charities is a great way to give back to your community and support organizations that are working to make a difference. Many charities accept donations of used electronics, which they then refurbish and donate to people in need or sell to raise funds for their programs.

When choosing a charity to donate to, consider the following:

- **Mission:** Choose a charity whose mission aligns with your values.
- **Transparency:** Choose a charity that is transparent about how it uses its donations.
- **Impact:** Choose a charity that has a proven track record of making a positive impact in the community.
- **Acceptable Items:** Check to see which specific devices a charity accepts.

Selling Online: Recouping Value and Finding New Homes

Selling your used electronics online is a great way to recoup some of your investment and find new homes for your devices. Online marketplaces, such as eBay, Craigslist, and Facebook Marketplace, provide a platform for connecting with potential buyers.

When selling used electronics online, follow these best practices:

- **Be Honest About the Condition:** Provide an accurate and detailed description of the device's condition, including any scratches, dents, or other cosmetic imperfections.
- **Take Clear Photos:** Take clear and well-lit photos of the device from all angles.
- **Price it Fairly:** Research the prices of similar devices on the market and price your device competitively.
- **Offer a Return Policy:** Offering a return policy can increase buyer confidence and help you sell the device more quickly.
- **Communicate Clearly:** Respond promptly and courteously to any questions from potential buyers.
- **Protect Your Privacy:** Wipe all personal data from the device before selling it. This includes deleting your accounts, clearing your browsing history, and erasing your contacts.

Trade-In Programs: A Convenient Option

Some manufacturers and retailers offer trade-in programs for used electronics. These programs typically offer a discount on a new device in exchange for your old device. Trade-in programs can be a convenient way to upgrade to a new device while ensuring that your old device is properly recycled or refurbished.

Preparing Your Devices for Donation or Sale: A Checklist

Before donating or selling your used electronics, be sure to follow these steps:

- **Back Up Your Data:** Back up any important data from the device to an external hard drive or cloud storage service.
- **Wipe Your Data:** Erase all personal data from the device. This is especially important for devices that contain sensitive information, such as smartphones, tablets, and computers.
- **Remove Your Accounts:** Remove all of your accounts from the device, such as your email account, social media accounts, and app store accounts.
- **Reset to Factory Settings:** Reset the device to its factory settings. This will erase all data and settings from the device and return it to its original state.
- **Clean the Device:** Clean the device to remove any dirt, fingerprints, or smudges.

- **Gather Accessories:** Gather any accessories that came with the device, such as chargers, cables, and manuals.

Case Study: A Phone's Second Life Supports a Community

A user upgraded to a new smartphone and decided to donate their old, but still functional, phone to a local charity. The charity refurbished the phone and donated it to a low-income individual who needed a reliable way to connect with family and access essential services. The phone not only provided a valuable resource for the individual but also helped the charity further its mission.

Giving your used electronics a second life through donation or sale is a responsible and rewarding choice. By following these guidelines, you can ensure that your devices continue to be useful while reducing e-waste and supporting worthy causes.

(11.3) Responsible Recycling Practices: Finding Certified Recyclers

When reuse is no longer an option, responsible recycling becomes the final, crucial step in the lifecycle of our electronic devices. However, "recycling" isn't always what it seems. A significant amount of e-waste is improperly processed, leading to environmental damage and health risks. This section will provide you with the knowledge to navigate the e-waste recycling landscape, ensuring your old electronics are handled ethically and sustainably. It's about becoming a conscious recycler, understanding the complexities of e-waste and making choices that protect both people and the planet.

The Dark Side of Recycling: A Global Problem

While recycling is often presented as a straightforward solution, the reality of e-waste recycling is far more complex. A significant portion of e-waste, particularly from developed countries, is exported to developing nations, where it is often processed in informal recycling operations with minimal environmental controls.

These operations often involve dismantling electronics by hand, burning circuit boards to recover valuable metals, and dumping hazardous waste in landfills or waterways. Workers, including children, are exposed to dangerous toxins, and the environment is contaminated with heavy metals and other pollutants. The documentary "The Story of Electronics" provides a powerful and disturbing look at the e-waste crisis.

Choosing a certified recycler is essential for preventing your e-waste from contributing to these harmful practices.

The Gold Standard: Understanding E-Waste Certifications

Certified recyclers adhere to strict standards for environmental protection, worker safety, and data security. Look for recyclers that are certified by one of the following organizations:

- **e-Stewards:** e-Stewards certification is considered the gold standard for e-waste recycling. e-Stewards recyclers are committed to preventing e-waste from being exported to developing countries and to protecting the health and safety of workers. They undergo rigorous audits and adhere to strict standards for data security and environmental protection.
- **R2 (Responsible Recycling):** R2 certification is another widely recognized certification program. R2 recyclers are committed to managing e-waste in an environmentally sound and socially responsible manner. They also undergo regular audits and adhere to standards for data security and worker safety.

When choosing a recycler, look for the e-Stewards or R2 certification mark on their website or promotional materials. You can also verify their certification status by visiting the e-Stewards or R2 websites.

Beyond Certification: Asking the Right Questions

While certification is a good starting point, it's also important to ask recyclers questions about their specific practices.

- **Where do you process the e-waste?** Make sure the recycler processes the e-waste in facilities that are located in countries with strong environmental regulations.
- **What are your data security practices?** Ask about how the recycler ensures that your data is securely erased from hard drives and other storage devices.

- **Do you export e-waste?** Make sure the recycler does not export e-waste to developing countries.
- **Do you use subcontractors?** If the recycler uses subcontractors, make sure that the subcontractors are also certified.

Data Security: Protecting Your Personal Information

Before recycling your electronic devices, it's crucial to protect your personal information. Even if you delete your files, your data may still be recoverable.

- **Overwriting:** The most effective way to erase data is to overwrite it with random data multiple times. There are several software programs that can be used to securely wipe your hard drive.
- **Physical Destruction:** For extremely sensitive data, you may want to consider physically destroying the hard drive. This can be done by drilling holes through the platters or shredding the drive.
- **Certified Data Destruction:** Some recyclers offer certified data destruction services. These services provide a guarantee that your data will be securely erased.

Case Study: A Data Breach Avoided Thanks to a Certified Recycler

A business owner was upgrading their company's computers and needed to dispose of the old machines. They chose a local recycler that claimed to be "environmentally friendly" but was not certified by e-Stewards or R2.

Unbeknownst to the business owner, the recycler was not properly wiping the hard drives. Some of the hard drives ended up in the hands of identity thieves, who were able to recover sensitive customer data.

This case illustrates the importance of choosing a certified recycler and verifying their data security practices.

Responsible recycling is not just about dropping off your old electronics at a collection center; it's about making informed choices that protect the environment, worker safety, and your personal data. By choosing certified recyclers and following proper data security procedures, you can ensure that your e-waste is handled responsibly and that you are contributing to a more sustainable future.

Chapter 12: Embracing Sustainable Electronics Practices

Welcome to Chapter 12, where we'll take a broader look at how our choices impact the electronics industry and the planet. It's not enough to simply repair our devices; we need to become active participants in creating a more sustainable system. This chapter is your guide to understanding the forces that shape the electronics industry and empowering you to make informed choices that promote repairability, longevity, and environmental responsibility. Think of this as becoming a conscious consumer, fighting for a future where electronics are designed to last and be easily repaired.

(12.1) Understanding Planned Obsolescence

Have you ever felt like your electronic devices are mysteriously designed to fail or become outdated just when you're getting comfortable with them? If so, you've likely encountered the effects of planned obsolescence. This deliberate strategy employed by many manufacturers involves designing products with a limited lifespan, encouraging consumers to purchase new versions more frequently. This section is dedicated to understanding this pervasive practice, helping you recognize its different forms and empowering you to make more informed choices. Think of it as pulling back the curtain on a hidden force that shapes our consumption habits.

The Mechanics of Short-Lived Devices: Unveiling the Tactics

Planned obsolescence is a multifaceted strategy employed to shorten the usable life of products. It's not always about intentionally making devices break quickly; it can also involve subtle techniques that encourage consumers to replace their devices even when they are still functional. Understanding these techniques is crucial for resisting their influence.

There are a few types of it as highlighted in the last chapter but let's dive into a few more,

- **Functional Obsolescence:** This is the most direct form of planned obsolescence. Products are designed with components that are likely to fail after a certain period of time. This can be achieved through the use of low-quality materials, fragile designs, or components that are deliberately difficult to replace. For example, batteries that are glued into smartphones make them difficult and costly to replace, encouraging consumers to buy a new phone instead.
- **Psychological Obsolescence:** This involves making products seem outdated or undesirable even when they are still functional. This can be achieved through the release of new models with only minor improvements, aggressive marketing campaigns that promote the latest features, or simply by changing the design or color scheme of the product. The constant barrage of new smartphone releases with incremental upgrades is a prime example of psychological obsolescence at work.
- **Systemic Obsolescence:** This occurs when a product is designed to be incompatible with newer technologies or systems. This can be achieved through proprietary connectors, software limitations, or a lack of support for new file formats or standards. For example, a printer that is no longer supported by the latest operating system becomes effectively obsolete, even if the printer itself is still functional.
- **Contrived Durability:** Some products may be made in ways that do not hold up as the product is used. This can be seen in phone screens.

The Motives Behind the Madness: Why Manufacturers Embrace Obsolescence

Planned obsolescence is driven by a desire to increase sales and profits. By shortening the lifespan of products, manufacturers can encourage consumers to purchase replacements more frequently, boosting their revenue and market share.

However, planned obsolescence also has some negative consequences:

- **Increased E-Waste:** Planned obsolescence contributes to the growing problem of e-waste, as consumers are forced to discard their devices more frequently.

- **Environmental Damage:** The manufacturing of new electronics requires the extraction of raw materials, the consumption of energy, and the use of hazardous chemicals. Planned obsolescence increases the demand for new electronics, exacerbating these environmental problems.
- **Consumer Frustration:** Consumers often feel frustrated and cheated by planned obsolescence, as they are forced to replace their devices more frequently than necessary.

Recognizing the Signs: Spotting Planned Obsolescence in Action

While it's not always easy to identify planned obsolescence, there are some telltale signs to look for:

- **Difficult to Repair:** The product is designed to be difficult or impossible to repair. Parts are glued together, screws are hidden or use proprietary heads, and repair information is not readily available.
- **Limited Support:** The manufacturer provides limited software updates or technical support for the product, making it difficult to use over time.
- **Constant Release of New Models:** The manufacturer releases new models with only minor improvements, creating a sense of psychological obsolescence.
- **Decreasing Battery Life:** Batteries are often a weak point in electronic devices. A battery that cannot be easily replaced and degrades quickly is a sign of planned obsolescence.

Case Study: Apple and the Slowdown Controversy

In 2017, Apple admitted to intentionally slowing down older iPhones to prevent unexpected shutdowns caused by aging batteries. While Apple claimed that this was done to improve the user experience, many consumers accused the company of using planned obsolescence to encourage them to upgrade to newer iPhones.

This case sparked a public outcry and led to several lawsuits against Apple. It also highlighted the ethical concerns surrounding planned obsolescence and the importance of transparency from manufacturers.

Understanding planned obsolescence is the first step in resisting this wasteful practice. By recognizing the tactics used by manufacturers, you can make more informed purchasing decisions and choose products that are designed to last. The following sections will show you the value of supporting the Right to Repair and making informed purchases.

(12.2) Supporting the Right to Repair Movement

We've established the importance of repair and the challenges posed by planned obsolescence. Now, let's delve into a powerful force fighting back: the Right to Repair movement. This global effort seeks to empower consumers and independent repair shops by ensuring access to the parts, tools, and information needed to fix our own electronics. It's about shifting the power dynamic and challenging manufacturers' control over the repair process. This section serves as your guide to understanding and supporting this crucial movement, empowering you to become an advocate for a more sustainable and equitable electronics ecosystem. Think of it as joining an army of fixers, fighting for the right to keep our devices alive.

What is the Right to Repair? A Fight for Ownership and Sustainability

The Right to Repair is based on the principle that consumers should have the right to repair the products they own, whether it's a smartphone, a tractor, or a medical device. This seemingly simple concept has far-reaching implications for consumers, businesses, and the environment.

The core tenets of the Right to Repair movement include:

- **Access to Parts:** Manufacturers should be required to make genuine replacement parts available to consumers and independent repair shops at a fair price.
- **Access to Tools:** Manufacturers should be required to provide access to the specialized tools needed to repair their products.
- **Access to Information:** Manufacturers should be required to provide access to service manuals, schematics, and diagnostic software.
- **No Software Locks:** Manufacturers should not be allowed to use software locks or other technological barriers to prevent repair.

The Arguments for Repair: Economic, Environmental, and Ethical

The Right to Repair movement is supported by a wide range of arguments:

- **Economic Benefits:** Repair creates jobs for independent repair technicians and stimulates local economies. It also saves consumers money by allowing them to repair their devices instead of replacing them.
- **Environmental Benefits:** Repair reduces e-waste and conserves resources by extending the lifespan of electronic devices.
- **Consumer Choice:** The Right to Repair empowers consumers to choose who repairs their devices and to make informed decisions about their purchases.
- **Innovation and Competition:** Independent repair shops can often offer innovative repair solutions that are not available from manufacturers. The Right to Repair fosters competition in the repair market, leading to lower prices and better service.
- **Ownership Rights:** Supporters argue that consumers should have full control over the products they purchase, including the right to repair them.

The Opposition: Manufacturers and Their Arguments

Despite the clear benefits of Right to Repair, many manufacturers actively oppose it, often citing concerns about:

- **Intellectual Property:** Claiming that providing access to repair information would infringe on their patents and trade secrets.
- **Safety:** Arguing that untrained individuals might injure themselves or damage the product during repair.
- **Quality Control:** Asserting that only authorized repair technicians can ensure quality repairs.
- **Security:** Claiming that giving repair information would compromise the security of the device.

However, Right to Repair advocates argue that these concerns are often exaggerated and used as a pretext to maintain a monopoly over repair services. They point out that independent repair shops often demonstrate high levels of expertise and professionalism, and that consumers are capable of making informed decisions about who repairs their devices.

The Battleground: Right to Repair Legislation Around the World

The Right to Repair movement is gaining momentum around the world, with legislation being considered or passed in several countries and states.

- **United States:** Several states have introduced or passed Right to Repair laws, focusing on different types of products, such as electronics, agricultural equipment, and automobiles.
- **European Union:** The European Union has implemented Right to Repair regulations for certain appliances, such as washing machines and refrigerators, and is considering expanding these regulations to other product categories.

Taking Action: How You Can Support the Movement

There are many ways to support the Right to Repair movement:

- **Stay Informed:** Follow organizations like iFixit, The Repair Association, and Public Knowledge to stay up-to-date on Right to Repair legislation and news.
- **Contact Your Legislators:** Write or call your elected officials to voice your support for Right to Repair laws.
- **Support Right to Repair Organizations:** Donate to or volunteer with organizations that are advocating for Right to Repair legislation.
- **Share Information:** Educate your friends, family, and colleagues about the importance of Right to Repair.
- **Vote with Your Wallet:** Support manufacturers that offer repairable products and fair repair policies.
- **Learn to Repair:** The more people who know how to repair electronics, the stronger the Right to Repair movement becomes.

The Right to Repair movement is a critical step towards creating a more sustainable, equitable, and innovative technology ecosystem. By supporting this movement, you can help empower consumers, promote environmental responsibility, and foster a culture of repair.

(12.3) Making Informed Purchasing Decisions

As consumers, we hold a significant amount of power to shape the electronics industry. Our purchasing decisions send a message to manufacturers, signaling what we value most in their products. By making informed choices that prioritize durability, repairability, ethical manufacturing, and energy efficiency, we can drive demand for more sustainable and responsible electronics. Think of this section as your consumer empowerment guide, helping you navigate the often-overwhelming world of electronics shopping and choose products that align with your values. It's about voting with your wallet for a more sustainable future.

Beyond the Hype: Focusing on What Matters Most

In today's marketing-saturated world, it's easy to get caught up in the hype surrounding the latest features and specifications. However, when it comes to making sustainable purchasing decisions, it's important to focus on what matters most:

- **Durability:** Durability is the key to extending the lifespan of your devices and reducing e-waste. Look for products that are made from high-quality materials and that have a reputation for reliability. Read reviews and look for information about the product's construction and build quality.
- **Repairability:** Choose products that are easy to repair and have readily available parts and information. Look for products with modular designs, easily accessible components, and online repair guides. Support manufacturers that embrace the Right to Repair.
- **Ethical Manufacturing:** Support manufacturers that are committed to fair labor practices, safe working conditions, and environmental responsibility. Look for companies that are transparent about their supply chain and that have certifications from organizations that promote fair labor practices.
- **Energy Efficiency:** Choose products that are energy-efficient to reduce your electricity consumption and lower your carbon footprint. Look for products with the Energy Star label.
- **Security and Longevity of Updates:** Many modern devices rely on regular software updates. Check the manufacturer's track record for providing updates and ensure that the product you are considering will be supported for the long term.

Practical Steps: Researching and Evaluating Products

Here are some practical steps you can take to make informed purchasing decisions:

1. **Read Reviews:** Read reviews from reputable sources to get an idea of the product's durability, performance, and reliability. Look for reviews that mention repairability and ease of maintenance.

2. **Check Repair Scores:** Some websites, such as iFixit, provide repair scores for electronic devices. These scores indicate how easy it is to repair the device.
3. **Look for Modular Designs:** Choose products with modular designs, where components can be easily replaced.
4. **Consider Refurbished Options:** Refurbished electronics offer a great way to save money and reduce your environmental impact. Refurbished products have been inspected, repaired, and restored to good working condition. They often come with a warranty, providing peace of mind.
5. **Ask Questions:** Don't be afraid to ask manufacturers or retailers questions about their products' durability, repairability, and ethical manufacturing practices.

Case Study: Fairphone - A Beacon of Sustainability

Fairphone is a smartphone manufacturer that is committed to sustainability and ethical manufacturing. Fairphone designs its phones to be durable, repairable, and modular. The company also uses responsibly sourced materials and pays its workers fair wages.

Fairphone is a shining example of how manufacturers can prioritize sustainability and ethical responsibility without sacrificing performance or quality.

Making informed purchasing decisions is a powerful way to influence the electronics industry and to create a more sustainable future. By choosing products that are durable, repairable, ethically manufactured, and energy-efficient, you can send a message to manufacturers that you value sustainability and responsibility.

Appendices

This section provides supplementary information to enhance your understanding and application of the concepts presented in this book. Think of these appendices as your toolkit companions, always there to provide a quick reference, a helpful resource, or a visual guide when you need them.

Appendix A: Glossary of Terms

This glossary provides definitions for common electronics terms used throughout the book. It's designed to be a quick reference guide to help you understand any unfamiliar terminology. While many terms have been explained in the body of the book, this Appendix provides a centralized and alphabetized list for easy access.

(Example Entries)

- **AC (Alternating Current):** An electrical current that periodically reverses direction, as opposed to direct current (DC) which flows in one direction only. Common in household electrical outlets.
- **Anode:** The positive terminal of a diode or other electronic component. Often marked with a '+' symbol.
- **Capacitance:** The ability of a capacitor to store electrical charge, measured in farads (F). Higher capacitance means more charge storage.
- **Continuity:** A complete and unbroken path for electrical current to flow. A multimeter's continuity test can quickly verify connections.
- **Diode:** An electronic component that allows current to flow in one direction only. Acts like a one-way valve for electricity.
- **ESD (Electrostatic Discharge):** The sudden flow of electricity between two electrically charged objects caused by contact, an electrical short, or dielectric breakdown. It can damage sensitive electronic components.
- **Flux:** A chemical cleaning agent that removes oxidation from metal surfaces, allowing solder to flow smoothly. Used in soldering.
- **Ground:** A reference point in a circuit that is typically connected to the earth. Provides a common return path for current.

- **IC (Integrated Circuit):** A miniature electronic circuit containing many components on a single chip. The "brain" of many electronic devices.
- **Ohm:** The unit of electrical resistance, named after Georg Ohm.
- **Polarity:** The positive or negative orientation of an electrical component or connection. Important for components like diodes and electrolytic capacitors.
- **Resistor:** An electronic component that resists the flow of electrical current. Used to limit current and divide voltage.
- **Schematic:** A diagram that shows the connections between the components in an electronic circuit. A roadmap for understanding electronic circuits.
- **SMD (Surface Mount Device):** An electronic component that is designed to be mounted directly onto the surface of a circuit board, without any leads extending through holes. Common in modern electronics.
- **Soldering:** The process of joining two metal surfaces together using molten solder. Creates a permanent electrical and mechanical connection.
- **Thermal Paste:** A heat-conductive compound applied between a CPU/GPU and heatsink to improve heat transfer. Prevents overheating.
- **Transistor:** An electronic component that is used to amplify or switch electronic signals and electrical power. A fundamental building block of modern electronics.
- **Voltage:** The electrical potential difference between two points in a circuit, measured in volts (V). Analogous to water pressure in a pipe.

Appendix B: Useful Resources (Websites, Forums, Suppliers)

This section provides a curated list of websites, forums, and suppliers that can help you further your knowledge and skills in electronics repair. These are resources I've found invaluable over the years, and I hope they prove useful to you as well.

(Example Categories and Entries)

- **Repair Communities and Forums:**

- o **iFixit (ifixit.com):** A comprehensive website with repair guides for a wide variety of electronic devices. User-submitted guides and teardowns are invaluable.
  - o **Electronics Repair School Forum:** A forum where you can ask questions and get help from other electronics enthusiasts. A great place to learn from others' experiences.
  - o **Electro-Tech-Online:** A vibrant online community dedicated to electronics. A wide range of skill levels are represented.
- **Component Suppliers:**
  - o **Digi-Key (digikey.com):** A large distributor of electronic components. Extensive selection and fast shipping.
  - o **Mouser Electronics (mouser.com):** Another large distributor of electronic components. Competitive pricing and a broad product catalog.
  - o **All Electronics Corp (allelectronics.com):** A good source for surplus and hard-to-find components. Great for finding unique and discounted parts.
- **Schematic and Datasheet Resources:**
  - o **AllDataSheet (alldatasheet.com):** A database of datasheets for electronic components. Essential for understanding component specifications.
  - o **Elektrotanya (elektrotanya.com):** A repository of service manuals and schematics. Often requires registration but provides access to valuable documents.
- **Tools and Equipment Suppliers:**
  - o **Amazon (amazon.com):** A convenient source for a wide variety of tools and equipment. Wide selection and competitive pricing.
- **Right to Repair Organizations:**
  - o **The Repair Association (repair.org):** Advocates for Right to Repair legislation. Stay informed on policy and advocacy efforts.

Appendix C: Troubleshooting Flowchart Examples

Flowcharts can be a helpful tool for systematically diagnosing problems. This section provides several examples of troubleshooting flowcharts for common electronic issues. These examples can be used as templates for creating your own flowcharts.

(Example Flowchart: Washing Machine Not Draining)

1. **Start:** Washing Machine Not Draining
2. **Check Drain Hose for Kinks or Blockages:** Is the drain hose kinked or blocked?
   - Yes: Straighten the hose or remove the blockage. Go to Step 6.
   - No: Go to Step 3.
3. **Check Drain Pump Filter for Debris:** Is the drain pump filter clogged with debris?
   - Yes: Clean the drain pump filter. Go to Step 6.
   - No: Go to Step 4.
4. **Test Drain Pump with Multimeter:** Is the drain pump receiving power and functioning properly?
   - Yes: Go to Step 5.
   - No: Replace the drain pump. Go to Step 6.
5. **Check Drain Valve:** Is the drain valve opening properly?
   - Yes: Consult a qualified technician.
   - No: Replace the drain valve. Go to Step 6.
6. **Test:** Run the washing machine. Is it draining properly?
   - Yes: End. Problem Solved.
   - No: Consult a qualified technician.

(Other Flowchart Examples)

- Laptop Overheating
- Smartphone Not Charging
- Computer Won't Turn On
- Display Has No Image

www.ingramcontent.com/pod-product-compliance
Lightning Source LLC
LaVergne TN
LVHW080117070326
832902LV00015B/2630